THE PARABLES we are about to consider may reveal that our religion, our wealth, and our culture have imprisoned us.

Jesus' parables are not innocent and neutral stories designed for momentary amusement.

He did not use parables to convey commonplace truth. Quite the opposite. He clothed His most radical ideas in the transparent garb of farmers, merchants, and field hands. The familiarity of the actors and actresses within these kingdom dramas disarmed Jesus' audience and set them up for His devastating message.

He lit a stick of dynamite, covered it over with an interesting story, and presented it to them. By the time these "good" people got these parables unwrapped, He and His disciples were a few miles down the road. Chances are they were still able to hear the explosion.

Properly understood, the parables can liberate us and lead us into the kingdom of God. Our lives can become a fresh incarnation of Christ's nature.

Cotton Patch Parables of Liberation

Clarence Jordan
Bill Lane Doulos

HERALD PRESS
Scottdale, Pennsylvania
Kitchener, Ontario

A Koinonia Publication

Scripture quotations, except where otherwise noted, are from *The Cotton Patch Version of Luke and Acts* (1969) and *The Cotton Patch Version of Matthew and John* (1970) by Clarence Jordan, used by permission of the publisher, Association Press.

Excerpts from *The Jerusalem Bible*, copyright 1966 by Darton, Longman and Todd, Ltd., and Doubleday and Company, Inc., are used by permission of the publisher.

COTTON PATCH PARABLES OF LIBERATION

Copyright © 1976 by Koinonia Partners, Inc.
Published by Herald Press, Scottdale, Pa. 15683
   Released simultaneously in Canada by Herald Press,
   Kitchener, Ont. N2G 4M5
   International Standard Book Number: 0-8361-1334-9
   Printed in the United States of America
   Design: Alice B. Shetler

10 9 8 7 6 5 4 3

To Florence and Sybil

Contents

Author's Preface

This book has been created, in many respects, by the people of Koinonia. Koinonia is a Greek word meaning fellowship, or community, and it designates a group of followers of Jesus who have resided for varying lengths of time on a farm near Americus, Georgia. Clarence and Florence Jordan and a few others founded Koinonia in 1942. Today it exists as an attempt to demonstrate the kingdom of God in the midst of an alien world.

The proclamation, teaching, and application of the gospel have engaged Koinonia in an expanding ministry that includes conducting discipleship schools; building houses and selling them at cost to poor families in southwest Georgia; running farm, food processing, sewing, and craft industries which provide jobs for the unemployed and profits for a Fund for Humanity; publishing and distributing books and records that communicate the radical ideas of Jesus Christ; and operating a preschool development center for neighborhood children. Throughout its diverse history Koinonia has consistently witnessed to three central gospel ideas: peace, brotherhood, and sharing.

Clarence died at the farm in the fall of 1969. [1] During over a quarter century he had provided a major share of the spirit and the muscle that gave birth to the present Koinonia. Both a Greek scholar and a farmer, Clarence divided his time between field work and book work. He translated most of the New Testament into the Cotton Patch version, a twentieth-century rendition, with a southern flavor, of the ancient texts. Many of his lectures were taped and have provided the material for records and a book, *The Substance of Faith and Other Cotton Patch Sermons.* [2]

Most of Clarence's teaching on the parables is included in this present volume. Clarence spoke before a variety of audiences, often without notes, and I have attempted in my editing to retain as much of the freshness of his spoken communication as possible.

As certainly as Clarence helped to build and inspire Koinonia, Koinonia helped to produce the incisive style and content of Clarence. During the several months that I have spent at the farm over the past few years, I have also been stimulated by the people here. All of them, past and present, have contributed to this book because they have contributed to my own spiritual growth. Several have assisted in specific ways through their encouragement and suggestions. Among these I owe particular thanks to Ladon Sheats, Al Zook, Suzanne Phillips, Florence Jordan, Larry Hesed, Erika Walton, Carolyn Mosley, and Sybil Doulos.

I have attempted to weave together the thoughts of Clarence and myself with excerpts from the Cotton Patch version (except where otherwise noted). Clarence's commentary is set apart from my own framework by italicized type, and his translations are immediately followed by the New Testament reference. Otherwise, I hope the reader is able to view this book as a natural whole.

Despite the extensive guidance of Clarence's writings, the worthy inspiration of the fellowship at Koinonia, and suggestions of those individuals listed above, I must assume final responsibility for the message and accuracy of the book.

Bill Lane Doulos
Koinonia Farm

Prologue

The parables of Jesus lead us into the kingdom of God. They come to us where we are, make use of the things and feelings that are familiar to us, transport us into an unfamiliar realm of values and relationships, and invite us to make ourselves at home.

For example, Jesus spoke once of a man who found a buried treasure. Jesus might have been imagining a tenant farmer out plowing in the owner's field when the blade of the plow struck a metal chest. This would not have been an unusual occurrence in Palestine, where centuries of invasions had forced families to hide their valuables underground. He uncovered the treasure, buried it again, and, in his excitement and joy, went off to sell all his possessions so that he'd have enough money to purchase the field.

Jesus said that this hazardous venturing was a good picture of the demands of the kingdom of God. This farmer risked all that he previously valued for the sake of his extraordinary find. And wherever the kingdom of God is discovered today men and women are leaving behind familiar patterns and pioneering a new existence.

This new existence is what the gospels, and the parables in particular, are all about. The very possibility of something new is liberating to many. How to recognize the treasure, how to respond to its presence, and how to permit it to refashion our whole way of living — these are the questions that Jesus answers by using His favorite teaching medium: the parable. And these are the questions that this book addresses.

Dorothy Kalins has written a book called *Cutting Loose — A Civilized Guide for Getting Out of the System.* [1] It speaks to corporation executives and their spouses who are disenchanted with the "rat race" — the familiar patterns. People who had been swallowed up by big salaries and social acceptance tell their stories of going to the country to begin more modest ventures, to do as they please, to live simply, to share life with their families.

Jesus, of course, also invites us to "cut loose." When he says, "Follow me," He is talking about a radical change overtaking us. But the shortcoming of Ms. Kalins' approach hinges on that word "civilized." Anything that is "civilized" can't be a guide for getting out of the system. For "civilization" and the "system" are intertwined, giving birth in turn to one another.

Among many other things, civilization has always brought war, exploitation, racism, and sexism. So what we need to help us "cut loose" is an "uncivilized" guide. We need to recognize an "uncivilized" Messiah walking toward us with His gift of the kingdom of God, asking us to order our lives along unfamiliar

14

lines. The kingdom which was the theme of Jesus' preaching and teaching is not a low-risk, blue-chip investment created by society for our consumption. It can't be calmly considered and casually digested. It can't be domesticated, nor can its leader be restrained from His continuous challenge to our way of life.

The parables bring us something new and wild. They are not meant to be interpreted to conform to our old polite ideas about what is good, acceptable, and "civilized." Jesus has His own ideas about what is good and acceptable.

I remember talking some years ago to an executive at a large university. He confided that he was disenchanted with his career. I rather brashly invited him to consider a career in Christian service, but I was left squelched and speechless by the insight of his response: "Why should I leave one rat race just to get into another?" He was a little too familiar with the "Christian service" industry, and he was looking for a more radical alternative than I could offer at the time. But there is nothing more radical than what Jesus offers, and that is the content of this book.

I used to work for Young Life, a Christian outreach organization that would welcome hundreds of first-time campers to its Colorado ranches each summer. The welcoming speech would almost always include these words: "For you campers who have never ridden a horse before, we have some good news. We have some horses here that have never been ridden."

In this book we have attempted to corral a few of the parables of Jesus. Clarence Jordan lends us his earthy translations and imaginative insights. And I offer a bit of my own horse sense, the best of which may be summed up as follows: some of these horses have never been ridden. So either put these parables on the shelf and return to your civilized existence, or prepare yourself as best you can for a rough ride. We may find ourselves landing together in some unpredictable places.

SHATTERING THE
STATUS QUO

The parables of Jesus help us to see two realities: the reality of a world whose values must be rejected, and the reality of a new world whose values must be accepted.

It is easy for us to live in a comfortable culture and to assimilate the values of the kingdom of God into a system produced, so the historians tell us, by our Judeo-Christian heritage. The American Jesus comes to us rather tamely, tidies up a few bad habits, makes us better citizens, and sends us back into a "civilization" that is grateful for our good influence. Everything flows smoothly. Christianity seems warm and right to us. There is no comprehensive discontinuity between what we have been and what we are or shall be. There is no rejection of traditional values, and, sadly, there is no entrance into the kingdom of God.

When we attempt to fit our Christianity into our culture, we are really attempting to fit a square peg into a round hole. We are trying to mix oil and water. Or we are trying to put new wine into old wineskins. The parables that say best what we must do when we encounter the kingdom — either by accident or after years of searching — are the twin parables found in Matthew 13:44-46.

The God Movement is like a man finding a treasure buried in a field. He covers it over again, and then with great excitement he sells all he owns and buys that field. Matthew 13:44.

Clarence put it like this:

The kingdom of God is like a man plowing in a field. He discovers a treasure, a box. He's plowing his old ox there. All of a sudden he hits something and he thinks it's a rock or a stump, and yet he sees it glitter like metal and he quickly throws his plow aside. He scratches around and finds it is a treasure box.

What does he do? Well, he might say, "You know, this is a very wonderful discovery I've got. I think I will go to school and write a PhD dissertation on treasure-hunting." But this isn't what he does. In his great excitement, this guy has the ability to decide on a clear-cut decisive course of action. He says, "I'm goin' to sell all I've got and buy that field."

He's got a sign up in the classified ads. "For Sale: one house; For Sale: one fiberglass boat; For Sale: this and that." He is goin' out of business. But is he? He's just gettin' ready to go into business. This man knows what he's doin'.

I think a lot of times we don't go into the

18

*kingdom business because we just aren't smart
businessmen. We want to hold on to our little
trinkets. We want to hold on to our status. Oh
yeah, we gotta keep our status. We can't be
fools for Christ. We can't give up our house.
So this guy is ready to sell out in order to
get this treasure of great price. This is the
kingdom; this is part of the revolution. And in
order to be in the revolution you many times
have to divest yourself of all earthly possessions.
You gotta make some adjustments in your
standard of living. And the adjustments that
Jesus generally calls on people to make are
not adjustments upwards but adjustments down-
wards.*

Also, the God Movement is like a jeweler looking for special pearls. When he finds a super-duper
one, he goes and unloads his whole stock and
buys that pearl. Matthew 13:45-46.

*Jesus said the kingdom is like a man seeking
goodly pearls. He finally sees one of great price.
He goes out and puts up a "Going-Out-of-
Business" sign on his shop and liquidates all
his lesser pearls in order to get that one of
great price. This is a parable that shows that
the call to the revolution is a drastic one,
calling for people to really reshape their lives,
their standard of living, their set of values, all
the things that they had thought were important. Out the door they go for this one, great,
consuming passion, the revolution which God
wants to usher in on this earth.*

19

These parables don't give us the specifics about what must be rejected, nor do they tell us the precise content of the new discovery. What they do tell us is that the discovery is so overwhelming that it shatters the routines that characterized our old way of living. The discovery can't be assimilated. Business can't go on as usual. *Jesus is not talking about reform, but about transformation.*

Two questions confront anyone who is serious about discipleship:

Have I discovered the treasure?

Chances are the treasure is very close — perhaps very familiar. We are like children playing with dynamite. Our problem is that we don't know what we've got hold of. We're in danger of spending our lives going to church, reading the Bible, saying our prayers, doing a few good deeds, being baptized and perhaps buried without being startled by the great discovery! Listen closely for the clink of the blade against the box.

Has the treasure reshaped my life?

Perhaps we really have made the discovery. Now the stakes are higher for us. We know that we cannot afford to be casual. Our energies and imaginations have been fired by a new affection. Is it conceivable that we could let the pearl slip through our fingers? That we could go on plowing until our excitement cools and our memory fades? That the status quo could survive?

OVERCOMING
OLD ALLEGIANCE

Jesus talked once about the varying responses to the kingdom of God. His conclusions are summarized in the parable of the farmer recorded in Matthew 13.

One day Jesus left the house and sat down on the seashore. Such a big crowd gathered around him that he got into a boat and sat down while the people stood on the beach. He told them many Comparisons: [1] "One time a farmer went out to plant. As he did so, some of the seeds fell on the path, and the birds came along and gobbled them up. Others fell on rocky places where the soil was shallow. Because they weren't planted deep they came up right away, but not having a deep root they withered when the hot sun hit them. Still others fell among the weeds, which grew up and choked them out. But others fell on good dirt and matured, some multiplying a hundred times, some sixty, and some thirty. Now please let *that* soak in." Matthew 13:1-9.

Now Matthew unravels this parable for us as follows: Everyone who hears the idea of the revolution and does not catch on, the evil one comes and snatches away what has been planted in his heart. This is the wayside seed. And the seed planted on the rocky shallow soil refers to the one who, when he hears the idea, right away he gets all hepped up about it. But he does not have any root within himself because he's wishy-washy. He soon gets tripped up. Now the seed which fell among the weeds was received by one who hears the idea, and the cares of this age and the deceitfulness of wealth choke out the idea and it becomes fruitless. But the one who is the deep earth, this is the one who hears the idea, and who understands it, and who brings forth abundant fruit. This is the parable of responses; the same idea, the same seed was planted in each instance. But the results were different.

Sometimes you preach to people and give them the Word, you read it to them from the Greek and the English; Phillips, King James, Revised Standard and New English Bibles, and they don't get it. It just goes in one ear and out the other, nothing in between to stop it. The people come in, they listen to the sermon, and as the preacher stands at the door they shake his hand and tell him what a fine sermon it was that they slept through, and that's the end of it. They're goin' about their business. It just never makes any contact, it never fires up anything. They're just there.

Then there are all those people who listen. You've got a crusade for Christ, you know, and you've got people listening and singing and getting all hepped and everybody comes down and makes a profession of faith in Christ. "Oh, ain't it wonderful!" But then, when the sailing gets rough, and when the persecution arises because of the Word — "Well nobody made it clear we were goin' to get persecuted. They just told us we were goin' to get a free ticket to heaven. What do you mean gettin' persecuted? That wasn't part of the contract." These are the shallow people.

And then there are those people who represent the good dirt, but they are preoccupied with other things. They're fine people. They're good-hearted people. They mean well. But they're just cut off from ever realizing their potential by the rat race, or whatever kind of race people are puttin' on now. The cares of the world, the distractions of this age, and the deceitfulness of riches (perhaps the most deceitful of all things is riches), these things just choke them out and prevent them from ever maturing.

Now it seems to me that this really classifies modern-day Christianity more than anything else. By and large, I think, Christians are good people. They're nice, middle class, suburban people. They're well-educated; they mean well. They don't hate Jesus! In fact, they love Him, if He'll stay in His place. And they don't mean Him any harm. It's just that they are so busy. They've got to go here; they've got to go there. They're busy with their houses; they're busy with their *automobiles; they're busy with their business. They just don't have time to think and they don't have time to get on the ball. So, they're choked out.*

But there are those who do bring forth fruit, some a hundredfold, some sixty, and some thirty.

Here again Jesus is hitting upon the idea that is so difficult for us to grasp, no matter how many times it's said and no matter how many ways it's phrased. The gospels are pointing a finger directly at us and saying the words that we don't want to hear: "Response to the kingdom means rejection of the traditional values that have shaped our lives."

We have been victimized by three attitudes that this parable lays bare. We may be like the seed upon the hard path, stripped of our capacity for growth and reduced to a short and meaningless existence. We have learned how to remain aloof. There is no room for response to anything new. We are amoral robots programmed by our culture to go about our business without emotion, and without the slightest possibility for making any delightful discoveries. Some of us, represented by the shallow soil, are seemingly the opposite, but the end result is the same. We have the capacity for immediate and impulsive response to the kingdom, but the fear of unknown consequences reveals that we, too, are robots. We don't have the stamina for the long haul or the perseverance for the hard times. Persecution is able to dehumanize us. And, finally, some of us are naive at the very point of Jesus' greatest concern, naive enough to think that we can maintain a foothold of respectability in both worlds, naive enough to suppose that material wealth and spiritual wealth can coexist. We want to embrace the values of two worlds because we don't understand that those two worlds are on a collision course.

The amazing truth of this parable is that the sowing of God's ideas does create obedient discipleship. There are some who do genuinely respond. The truth penetrates our hardness, overcomes our fears, and destroys our old allegiance. The kingdom takes root in our lives and brings forth an abundance of faith-fulness.

I remember breezing along the Pennsylvania Turnpike a few years back, and the status quo for me at that time was about 70 miles per hour. I passed countless signs that said that 65 was the maximum, but they made no impression. Then I came to a larger billboard that portrayed a fist with a forefinger pointing squarely in my direction. The caption in letters several feet high read: "YOU, SLOW DOWN." My foot instinctively went to the brake for fear this hand was going to reach out literally and grab me. I was seeing those speed limit signs, but they weren't registering. If they had sunk in, not being a foolish or reckless person, I would have slowed down. But the Pennsylvania State Police had to draw me a convincing picture.

So it is with Jesus, trying to shock us awake with the reality of our situation, and with the crucial nature of the opportunity confronting us. He comes to us in parables because we have a tendency to look without seeing and listen without hearing or catching on. The passage from Isaiah that Matthew quotes in connection with this use of parables applies to us:

> They strain their ears and never catch on;
> For the hearts of these people are hard,
> And their ears are dull,
> And their eyes are dim.
> Otherwise, their eyes might see,
> And their ears might hear,
> And their hearts might understand,
> And they might turn around,
> And I'll make them well. Matthew 13:14-15.

Jesus draws us pictures — He stages little dramas for us — because He wants to make us well. But it almost seems that there is something in us that doesn't want to understand. We want to hold to the death-dealing systems that Jesus has come to smash. These systems may impose upon us a job, an income level, a social milieu, or a lifestyle that keeps us enslaved to its own preservation at the same time that it keeps us too busy to accept an invitation to a greater feast — one that Jesus talked about in Luke 14:

> One time a man gave a big dinner, and he sent invitations to many people. When everything was on the table, he sent his servant

26

around to all the guests saying, "Y'all come, it's all ready." But one after another began to beg off. The first one said, "I have bought a tract of land, and I've just go to go look it over. If you will, please excuse me." And another said, "I have bought five teams of mules, and I simply must go and try them out. If you will, please excuse me." Another said, "I just got married, and therefore I *cannot* come!" So the servant returned and told his boss what had happened. Then the boss had a fit, and said to his servant, "Run out real quick into the streets and alleys of the city, and bring in here the poor and the disabled and the blind and the crippled." After a while his servant announced, "Sir, I've done what you told me, but the table still isn't full." The boss then said to the servant, "Well, go out on the highway and sidewalks and collar them to come on in here, so I'll have a full table. Because I'm telling you a fact, not one of those guys who got an invitation will get a taste of my food." Luke 14:16-24.

Jesus was trying to show that the kingdom of the new order, this family of the Father, is like a big family gathered around the table, eating together. It's fellowship. It's fun. It's feasting. It's joy. It's life. It's beauty. But there is also a tragedy involved. There are some people who choose not to attend. Jesus' picture of going to hell was not being sent to a place of torment, but just being left out of the joy of the fellowship.

Jesus began, "There was a certain man who made a great supper, a big banquet." Now we know that this man represents God. God

27

made a big banquet, and that's the kingdom, and he invited a lot of folks. And he sent his slave out, at the hour of the supper, and he said to those who had been invited, "Y'all come; it's all ready." And they, beginning with the very first one, began to beg off. The first one said, "I have bought me a farm, and I got to go look it over. I beg you, please have me excused." Now this fellow is saying, "I'd like to come to your banquet. I know you're going to have some mighty good stuff. I heard about that barbecue you make, and it's very, very nice, and I'd like to be there for it. But I bought me a piece of land."

Now this word "land" to the Jews was a powerful idea. To buy a piece of the Holy Land meant to be a part of a nation of people. The man and the land were, somehow tied up together. You really had a corner on God if you had a little piece of God's land that you could own. Every devout Jew wanted to own — if it wasn't but just a few square inches — a bit of his native soil. And this, I think, was Jesus' way of symbolizing nationalism and patriotism.

And so, this fellow is saying, "Well, I want to come, but I don't agree with this idea of yours that you let anybody in there, no matter where they're from. We've got to think of the kingdom in terms of America. And America is for the Americans, you know. We can't let these other folks be part of the inheritance. So I'm going to hold on to my little piece of land. I've got to look it over." Super-

28

patriotism! It keeps people out of the bound-less kingdom of the Spirit.

And then, another one said to him, "I have bought me five yoke of oxen, and I got to go try them out. I beg you, will you please have me excused?" Now this is an interesting kind of thing: "I have bought me five teams of mules," we might say. In Jesus' day, folks didn't have a two-car garage, but they all had at least one yoke of oxen. The yoke of oxen was a sort of detachable power unit. You could hook 'em up by day, and plow with 'em, and then hook 'em up to the cart at night and go courting with 'em. It was sort of a combination jeep and tractor affair. It was a power unit that you could get various attachments for. And nearly every family had at least one yoke of oxen. And there were some rich folks out in the suburbs that even had two. But, here's a guy who's got five yoke of oxen! What's he doing with so many jeeps? I don't know, but unless I miss my guess, this old fellow was a used ox dealer. He'd been to the auction, and bought him several yoke of them. And he had them over in the barn, polishing up the toenails, and grooming up the horns, and combing the tails, and getting them all ready to put out in the showroom the next day. That's what he was going to do with them.

This man was all business. He was a free-wheeling, free enterprise, capitalistic businessman and he said, "Sure, I'd like to go along with you in this enterprise, but I've got to make some money. I've got to open

29

up early in the morning there. I belong to the Ox Associates. We've got chains of ox dealers all over this country. They transferred me. I'm area supervisor of the ox dealers in this section here and if the corporation told me to go to Timbuktu on an ox deal, I'd go down there."

The other man said, "I have married a woman, therefore, I can't come." He just said "therefore." It wasn't any use to ask to be excused. He was told to be home by six o'clock. He wasn't going to that banquet.

Now what does this man represent? He is just simply saying, "I'm not going to break with my wife," who is the symbol of all family relationships. She is the symbol of all the ties, rising above friends, above relatives, and even above families. He is saying, "I just don't want to belong to a movement that's going to break up my family, that is going to put me at odds with my parents and my brothers and sisters. I admire the movement and I think it's got some good things, but I just don't feel that I can sacrifice my friends and my relatives for my convictions. I'm just honestly going to tell you so. I can't be there."

The slave came back and reported all these refusals to his lord, and the master was angry, and he said to his slave, "Well, run out quickly to the streets and alleys of the city, and bring in here the poor folks, and the crippled, and the lame, and the blind." And his servant went out and gathered them all together, and he came back and he said, "Master, what you told me to do has been done, and there's still some room around the table." And the master said to the slave, "Well, then run out to the country, and get the country folks, and bring them in here, so that my house might be full. I want to tell you," he said, "not one of those guys who was invited shall eat of my supper."

In this parable we have a description of what the kingdom is, what keeps us out, and the dangers of refusing our opportunity to participate. Old allegiance must fall if we are to give an adequate response to God's invitation.

3

REACHING OUT
FOR LIBERATION

We're beginning to get the picture that Jesus is using these parables to shake us loose — to get us to open our eyes. There are things in our lives that we have always thought were good ingredients for kingdom citizenship. We participate in some time-honored institutions, we might even say some "sacred" institutions. God takes his proper place alongside family, country, and occupation.

But what if God is demanding more than His "proper" place? What do we do when God loses His civility, when He withdraws His blessing from middle-class American values? What happens when we must choose *between* God and social relationships, *between* God and country, *between* God and mammon? There is no doubt that these choices come to us. The parable of the great feast is reaching out to grab us. But we may think that the decision is not urgent. We are wrong.

There is one parable in particular that emphasizes the critical nature of taking immediate action in view of impending circumstances. This is a crisis parable. The parable itself is found in Luke 12:58-59, but it is particularly helpful to quote the context beginning at verse 49.

"I came to kindle a fire on the earth, and what wouldn't I give if it were already roaring! I have an ordeal to go through, and how pressed I am until it comes to a head! Do you all think that I came to give the world peace? No, I tell you, not peace but conflict. From now on, if a house has five people in it, they shall be fighting — three against two and two against three. A father will be against his son, and the son against his father; a mother against her daughter, and the daughter against her mother; a mother-in-law against the bride, and the bride against her mother-in-law."

He said to the crowd, "When you see a cloud blowing in from the west, right away you say, 'Here comes a rain,' and sure enough, it does rain. And when the south wind is blowing you say, 'It's gonna be hot,' and hot it is. You phonies, you are skilled at weighing scientific facts, but how is it that you can't interpret the signs of the times? And why can't you tell what's right for you? For example, when you're going to court with a man, wouldn't it be better to make an effort to settle out of court rather than having him drag you before the judge, and the judge rule against you, and deliver you into the custody of the warden, and the warden slap you into the pen? I'm telling you, you won't get out of there till you've paid through the nose." Luke 12:49-59.

We seldom think of Jesus as coming to kindle

a fire on earth, to bring conflict, yet wherever Jesus went He seemed to precipitate awkward situations and often crisis situations. The upshot of His ministry was crucifixion. Jesus passes on to us the crisis and He asks, "Why can't you tell what's right for you?" What's right for us is (1) to recognize the crisis, the fire that is about to consume us, the imprisonment that is about to rob us of our freedom, and (2) to respond before it is too late.

We are in a crisis, and we must act swiftly, and that is the virtue of the man on his way to court. He is able to perceive that his time has come, that his freedom must either be seized by immediate action, or lost. There is no more breathing room. He has maintained the semblance of freedom, but now judgment is about to fall. [1] He has nurtured the naive hope that some evidence would turn up to acquit him, but now he must take an extraordinary step: he must strike a last-minute bargain with his accuser. Far better for him to swallow his pride than to lose his freedom.

This parable is designed to impress upon us one thing: the urgent need for decisive action. The kingdom of God is upon us. Our liberation is at stake.

The truth of our own situation is that we too are on our way to prison each time we reject the overtures of the kingdom. If we do not understand that a fire has been kindled, if we have not been electrified by what's happening in our lives and in our world, then we have accepted a personal destiny that can-

34

not liberate us. We are experiencing an imitation freedom, but all the doors that lead to life, to joy, to a fearless quest for wholeness for ourselves and our world, all these doors are being bolted shut by our apathy and fear. To enter the kingdom is not to enter a restrictive network of do's and don't's. It is to escape such confinement for the sake of a limitless expanse of spiritual abundance.

Sometimes we are more afraid of what freedom *might* mean for us than of what bondage *does* mean for us. The status quo and the old allegiance are the bread and water we are tempted to accept as our regular prison fare — unless the truth of our circumstances and of God's calling can get through to us, and unless we act decisively upon that truth. "The truth will liberate you," if you are an "honest follower" of truth. [2] The remainder of this book will be concerned with "truth" and with "following" where Jesus, through His parables, leads us.

But why all this talk of crisis? Of urgency? Of the need for immediate action? Why all this incompatibility between who we are and who God is asking us to be? We must remember now that we are trying to see the parables simply and clearly, and to do this we must try as best we can to leave behind our presuppositions about what is normal Christian experience. The parables are not innocent and neutral stories designed for our momentary amusement or to confirm a commonsense approach to spiritual

development. This is not "story time" but
"life-changing time." And in this sense the
parables are very much a part of the total life
and teaching of Jesus. The fact is that Jesus
was a revolutionary. We do not have space to
lay out the massive evidence that supports this
contention, other than to point out the obvious:
Jesus was crucified. Storytellers don't get crucified. Yet it was a parable that led Jesus right
to the brink of destruction. [3]

So if anyone is rocking the boat it is hopefully Jesus. And we should not be surprised, if
we are to judge by His past behavior patterns,
that Jesus is once again shattering the pretenses
of good religious folk.

We have difficulty with the ideas of urgency
and discontinuity. We are much more at home
with slow contemplative processes of gradual
reform. We tend to see Jesus as the source of
a broad, generous, and accommodating invitation to come along into the kingdom by a process of osmosis rather than metamorphosis.
"Follow me" has lost its abrasive ring. But, in
reality, much to our dismay, the gospels speak
of kingdom entry as a "narrow" proposition.
Simple familiarity with Jesus does not qualify
one for admission.

Clarence gives us the following translation and
commentary on Luke 13:22-30. [4]

*Now Jesus was going along from city to
city and preaching in the villages, making His
journey to Jerusalem. Then somebody said to
Him, "Lord, are just a few being rescued?"*

36

And He said to them, "You put all you've got into entering through the narrow gate, because many, I tell you, will do their utmost to get in but just won't make the grade."

And then He tells this story: "When the householder has gotten up and locked the door, then those on the outside will begin to stand and knock at the door saying, 'Master, open up for us.' And then He will answer and say to them, 'I don't know where you come from.' Then they will begin to say, 'Well, we ate with You and we drank with You and You taught up and down in our streets. And then He will say, 'I just don't recognize you at all. Get away from Me, you religious gangsters.'

"Out there (that is, on the outside) there will be weeping and grinding of teeth, when you will see Abraham and Isaac and Jacob and all the prophets in the family of the Father, but you, yourselves, cast out. And they will come from the east and west and from the north and south, and they will gather around the table in the family of the Father. And I want to tell you that those who are on the bottom will be on top, and those who are on top will be on the bottom."

I doubt if many of us have seen ourselves as outsiders in terms of the family of the Father. Perhaps we should take another look. Jesus gives us on several occasions, often connected with His parabolic discourse, this simple guideline: "Those who are on the bottom will be on top, and those who are on the top will be on the bottom." [5] Sometimes we wish the parables were more complex and obscure! But taking this statement at face value, it should be a warning to anyone caught reading this book. People who read books, particularly people who read religious books, thereby possess some of the trademarks of middle-class "religious gangsterism." [6] This warning goes double for people who write books! There is not enough evidence here to convict you, but if you continue reading, this book may begin to sound like your indictment. (If you stole this book, or borrowed it from a friend, you may breathe a slight sigh of relief.)

This idea that the last shall be first and the first last is repeated so often in the gospels that it has become trite and commonplace. But it is a startling truth when we put it into the context of economics, social prestige, military might, and religious elitism. Jesus did not choose the parables to convey commonplace truth. Quite the opposite. He clothed His most radical ideas in the transparent garb of farmers, merchants, and field hands. The familiarity of the actors and actresses within these kingdom dramas disarmed Jesus' audience and set them up for His devastating message. Clarence explained the procedure this way:

A parable is something you use when the situation is very dangerous. You hide your truth in it; it's sort of a literary Trojan horse. Now, you know what a Trojan horse is? You've read in Greek history of how Helen

38

was captured, and she was taken captive into the city of Troy, and all of her kinsmen went out to rescue her. They camped around Troy where she was held and they besieged it and they battered it and they couldn't take it. And finally some fellow had a bright idea. They built this great big ol' wooden horse and put a few men inside of it, and then all the other people went away. And the folks up on the wall looked out and they didn't see anybody out there — nothin' but this great big wooden horse — and they said, "Well, those guys have just given up and they've gone. But look at the thing they've left."

So they opened up the gates and they all went out there and, "Well, that's a fine ol' horse. Maybe we could take him into town and build a big merry-go-round to go with him, and we'll just have a wonderful thing." They were looking and looking, but they didn't see anything; they were listening and listening, but they didn't hear anything. And so they got them a jeep and pulled that ol' horse into the city, not knowing what they were doing. You see, the real thing was hidden inside. They weren't aware of what was happening. So they pulled it on past the gates to right where those Greeks had wanted to go all along. And they put the horse on exhibit, all day, and let the school out so the children could see him. But late that night, about two o'clock, when everybody was asleep, the little trap door on that horse opened up, and the men came out. They rushed to the gates of the city, opened them up, and by that time, all the soldiers had come 'round. The soldiers came in and took the city.

Now Jesus used that kind of a Trojan horse technique under certain circumstances. He used it when the situation was dangerous, and when His hearers were difficult. When they would just stop up their ears and shut their eyes, and they wouldn't hear and they wouldn't see, Jesus would bring out a Trojan horse to ram it through their ears and get it beyond their blind eyes.

This wasn't a new technique for Jesus at all. Others had used it. You remember that Nathan the prophet used it on King David.[7] King David was up in his palace one day, way up on top of his roof, and he looked out and he saw next door a beautiful young lady taking a sun bath. And he asked somebody to please find out her name and telephone number, and they came back and told him that she was Mrs. Uriah the Hittite. "Oh, Mrs. Uriah the Hittite, huh? Mmmm . . . too bad. Oh," says David, "would you please call the local draft board and have Mr. Uriah classified 1-A, and have him put on the front lines?"

Pretty soon there was the inevitable government telegram informing Mrs. Uriah that she was a widow. Then a little later there was a wedding, and King David married the widow.

Now this infuriated Nathan the preacher. He wanted to say something to David about that. Now if he'd been like John the Baptist and followed the Baptist tradition, things would have gone badly for him. You remember when Herod

40

took his brother's wife, John the Baptist went running in there and said, "What do you mean taking your brother's wife?" And ol' Herod said, "Put that little Baptist preacher in the clink." So he got locked up, you see; he wasn't wise. But Nathan knew he might get put in the jug if he went in with that kind of thing.

So he went to King David one day and he said, "King David, I got a little problem."

"What's your problem, Reverend? You buildin' an educational plant and need a little money?"

"No sir, no sir, not that."

"Well then, do you need a new mimeograph machine?"

"No sir, I don't need that. My problem is that I've got two church members that are giving me a little trouble."

Now King David was not suspicious of anything. He didn't know what was going on.

Nathan continued, "I've got two church members giving me a little trouble. One of them is a very rich man with a lot of sheep. And another member of my church is a very poor man, with just one sheep. Well, King David, the rich member had somebody come visit him, and instead of going out to his flock and getting one of his sheep and killing it to have a little barbecued lamb, he goes and gets the only sheep my poor member's got and kills it for himself."

Now King David got so mad, he said, "Who is that kind of fellow? Show him to me; I'll sure fix him up."

Well, you see, David had pulled it in; he'd

pulled it past his gate, on into the inside, and Nathan unlocked the door, pointed at David, and said, "You ask me who the man is? THOU ART THE MAN!"

King David had passed judgment on himself. There wasn't anything he could do then but go out and write another psalm.

Many of the parables that follow will be Trojan horse parables. As you come to understand them, you will find yourself in jeopardy. Perhaps you have already been threatened by the parables of the farmer sowing his crop and the great feast. Do you identify with one of the three varieties of nonproductive soil? Are you one of the guests who made excuses? Who or what controls *you*?

I have shared several insights now that might be unwisely used to shield you from the incisive truth of the parables we are about to consider: Beware of the innocent story. Beware of the Trojan horse. Beware of the easy self-assurance that protests, "But we are the children of Abraham." This book is not an attempt to entrap you, but to set you free. Our only hope for liberation is to see God as He truly is, and to see ourselves as He must see us. If you construct your defenses in advance so that you can duck when the punch of the parables comes your way, then you are the loser. The parables are a means of treading softly until the climactic scene unveils the villains and the heroes.

Unfortunately, most of my readers, unlike

Jesus' audience, are already acquainted with the plot. We already know that the wealthy and the "righteous" turn out to be the bad guys, and the Samaritans, tax collectors, and other assorted prodigals turn out to be the good guys. So there is no point in trying to maintain suspense. My only hope is to be straightforward, to plead with you from the beginning to permit yourself to be "set up." "Thou art the man!" Let us begin with that assumption. Jesus is leveling a shotgun loaded with accusation at many of us. If we acknowledge the truth of our indictment, there is still hope for us as there was for the panic-stricken defendant on his way to court.

But before we consider our hope (Chapter Eight), let us consider our predicament. The kingdom of God has come. We have not acted decisively. We have not abandoned our stand-pat lives. And we have striven mightily to maintain our priority position in secular affairs against all kingdom-comers. We have not reached out to grasp our freedom. Indeed, if we are honest, the parables we are about to consider may reveal that our religion, our wealth, and our culture have imprisoned us.

GOD AGAINST THE CHURCH!

The true children of God are the children who carry with them the nature of the Father. It is impossible, therefore, to separate the parables that tell us about God from those that speak about discipleship. As we look at who God is we pick up essential clues about who we're supposed to be.

One thing that needs to be made clear before we begin: we can't change the nature of God, but the nature of a man or woman can be changed. The possibility of human conversion is an inherent part of the good news. Some of us may be confused at this point. We think that the good news is that *God* can be changed so that we can avoid having to change our own lives. But the parables don't give us a choice about who God is, they only give us a choice about who we are going to be.

Clarence recounts the following story about the time when Koinonia, the "integrated" farm community he founded in southern Georgia, was having a good deal of trouble with its "Christian" neighbors. He begins by making the point that membership in God's family is optional, not automatic.

I don't think Jesus taught that everybody was a child of God. He did not teach that ALL men are brothers. He taught that all men COULD be brothers. And he didn't teach that ALL people are children of God. He said all COULD be children of God. [1] Now this is a vital point, because there's so much tommy-rot goin' around today about the brotherhood of man.

And there's a lot of tommy-rot goin' on about integration. Now, I know that the church of God does not respect color lines, but its aim is not integration. People say, "Well, you know, we have to learn to live together here on earth 'cause you know heaven is integrated." Sure. Heaven's integrated. Hell is too. They're both integrated. Integration isn't the difference between heaven and hell.

I went to see a Baptist deacon out our way, to see if he wouldn't sell us some ground limestone to go on our land. Our land's rather acid, and to grow clover or legumes you have to put about a ton of ground limestone on each acre. We wanted to plant about a hundred acres of clover. So we asked this Baptist deacon who had a limestone agency if he would spread a hundred tons of limestone on our land. By that time, the violence of the mid-fifties had subsided. Nobody was shootin' at us or blowin' up our homes. We thought maybe this deacon would like to sell us a little lime.

So he said, "Well, Mr. Jordan, I appreciate

your askin' me and offerin' me that business 'n all like that. But to tell you the truth, I'm scared."

I said, "Well, I'm scared too. But who are you scared of?"

"Well," he said, "I'm scared to tell you who I'm scared of?"

"Man, you ARE scared! Well what are you scared of?"

"I'm scared that if I do business with you they might blow up my trucks."

And I said, "Yeah, I think they might. They are right handy with dynamite. I wouldn't doubt it at all. But, in times past, Christians have been called upon to lose not only their businesses, but, if need be, their heads."

"Yeah," he said, "I read about that."

"You don't wanna be a part of it?"

"Noooo," he said, "not me!"

"Well, I guess I'll have to be going." So I started to leave and he called me back.

He said, "Say, come here. Maybe we can work out some way for you to get that lime."

And I thought, here's a Christian who's gonna be a man. He's gonna stand up and be counted. He isn't gonna be one of those kind that, when persecution arises, he withers away. Maybe he's gonna stand up and bear a little fruit. Maybe a hundred tons of lime! I don't know. So I went back in.

He said, "Uh, I think maybe I can sell you that lime if you'll make a public statement that you folks no longer believe in integration, and have that statement printed in the Americus Times Recorder." *That's our little daily paper.*

I said, "Now, my dear friend, we didn't come in here to trade our souls. We came in here to buy lime. But, you got us wrong. We never have from the beginning said we believe in integration."

He said, "What you believe in?

"All we've ever said is that God is no respecter of persons, that there's no white and black in the household of God."

"Good God A'mighty, that's integration, ain't it?"

"No sir, that isn't integration," I said. "That's the nature of God. And I don't see any point in us puttin' a little ad in the Americus paper that God ain't what He used to be. In the first place, I don't think God would even see it. He gets the Atlanta Journal. But assuming that He did see it, I don't think it'd make much impression on Him. Looky here. We haven't been able to change even the Supreme Court, and I think God's more bullheaded than those Supreme Court justices. And if we can't change the Supreme Court, how do we ever change God? Maybe we just have to make up our minds to get along with God and just cooperate with Him and let Him be what He is."

Well, you know, we didn't get our lime. Still haven't got it. But God's still no respecter of persons.

In this book we're hopefully going to shelve

47

our attempts to refashion God in our own image. We're going to concentrate on the original God, keeping in the back of our minds the possibility that He hasn't changed much over the past 2,000 years.

Three of the most familiar parables reveal to us the essence of this original God, and they happen also to be among the most explosive of Jesus' stories. They appear to speak about a sheep, a coin, and two sons, but they really concern the nature of the Father. Clarence gives a full analysis of each story following his translation.

Now all the "nigger-lovers" and black people were gathering around him to listen. And the white church people and Sunday school teachers were raising cain, saying, "This fellow associates with black people and *eats* with them." So Jesus gave them this Comparison:

"Is there a man among you who, if he has a hundred sheep and loses one of them, will not leave the ninety-nine in the pasture and go hunt for the lost one? And when he finds it, he joyfully puts it on his shoulders and goes home with it. He calls over to his friends and neighbors, 'Hey, y'all, I found my lost sheep. Isn't that wonderful?' I'm telling you, in the same way there'll be more joy among the spiritually sensitive ones over a single 'outsider' who reshapes his life than over the ninety-nine 'righteous' people who don't need to change their ways." Luke 15:1-7.

The whole new order of the spirit is going to ride on our concept of God. What kind of platform does He have? What does He want to see accomplished? All of Jesus' ethics were rooted deeply in the nature of God. He didn't say, "Love your enemies and give 'em fits." He didn't say, "Love your enemies because that is the best strategy." He said, "Love your enemies that you might be children of your Father." This is the starting point for these parables in Luke 15.

The text says that when this fellow finds his lost sheep he takes it home with him. He brings that little lost sheep right into the living room and says, "Hey, I got my sheep!" And his wife says, "Get that sheep out of my living room. He's going to mess. Get out! I just vacuumed in here!"

Now this is a crazy thing for a man to do with a lost sheep. But he's so happy he's got it, and he brings it in, and even though it's making a stink he says, "I want him in my living room. Here's my lost sheep and I've found him." Do we get the point? Jesus is saying that God Almighty is that kind of God. He goes a little bit further and He says, "There will be more joy over this outsider than over ninety-nine good church members."

Or suppose a woman has ten pennies [2] and loses one of them; won't she get the flashlight and a broom and sweep and look carefully till she finds it? And when she does find it, she calls over to her friends and neighbors and says, "Hey, y'all, you know that penny I lost? Well, I found it. Isn't that nice?" In the same way, I tell you, there's a rejoicing on the part of God's faithful ones over a single 'outsider' who re-shapes his life. — Luke 15:8-10.

The *drachma* was the smallest of all the coins used in Jesus' day. It would be our penny. And this woman had ten of them and she lost one.

Now, I don't know about all this, but here's what I'm guessing. I'm guessing that these pennies had a sentimental value. They were part of a necklace that this lady had. Back in those days, when you got married, you didn't give a woman a ring — you gave her a neck-lace to put around her neck. I would guess that this woman had caught her broom handle in her wedding necklace and broke it. The coins just went every which way and she found nine of them but she couldn't find one of them.

It says she lit a lamp, and that she took some coal oil, and she got a broom and swept and swept and swept until she found it. She prob-ably wore out a fifty-cent broom for a one-cent piece. Now what kind of economy is that? Well, it wasn't the value of the penny. The hero of this parable is not the penny. All it did was just roll away and get lost. This isn't the parable of the lost coin, this is the parable of the sweeping woman. And it isn't so much the actual cash value of that penny — it's the senti-mental value, the love associated with it.

My wife's got some chinaware, and it's very precious to her because we got it for our wed-ding. And we get it out when we have company. On one such occasion I was doing my chore of washing dishes, and she said, "Be careful, Honey." And I kept washing and in a little while I broke a cup. And then everything got real quiet. Now, I'm used to the storm, but it's the calm before the storm that bothers me. I kinda thought I'd better look around and reconnoiter and see what the situation was and I found my wife in a very sad mood.

"Now listen," I said, "I'll get ya another one; don't take it so hard."

She said, "You can't get anymore." They were out of print or out of bake, or whatever you call china. "They don't make 'em anymore."

Well, the little ol' cup probably wasn't worth but a quarter; it wasn't worth crying over, but it had sentimental value. It was part of a set. And she didn't want the set broken.

And I think this is what Jesus is saying about God. Every little human being in this world is part of God's set. And God just has a sentimental attachment for his set, for all of humanity. God doesn't go by the kind of arithmetic that you and I go by. He has never learned to deal in fractions. God didn't get that far in school. I think He's like my father who had ten children, and many a time I thought, "Well, my goodness, with a family this big, Daddy can't love me very much. I can only claim one tenth of his love." But my father loved me with all of his love. It's just that way with love. There is no fraction in it.

You can't break it up into pieces. And God wants the whole human race. He just can't deal in fractions.

And so Jesus is saying to these people who were griping and mumbling and grumbling about the fact that He was taking in all kinds of people, bums and drunks and the poor folks and everybody, He was saying, "Well, I just can't help it. God just has a sentimental attachment for His people. And, whether you like it or not, God loves 'em, and it does seem to me that if they're precious in God's sight, they ought to be precious in yours, too."

He went on to say, "A man had two sons. The younger one said to his father, 'Dad, give me my share of the business.' So he split up the business between them. Not so long after that the younger one packed up all his stuff and took off for a foreign land, where he threw his money away living like a fool. Soon he ran out of cash, and on top of that, the country was in a deep depression. So he was really hard up. He finally landed a job with one of the citizens of that country, who sent him into the fields to feed *hogs!* And he was hungry enough to tank up on the slop the hogs were eating. Nobody was giving him even a hand-out.

"One day an idea bowled him over. 'A lot of my father's hired hands have more than enough bread to eat, and out here I'm starving in this depression. I'm gonna get up and go to my father and say, "Dad, I've sinned against God and you, and am no longer fit to be called your son — just make me one of your hired hands."'

"So he got up and came to his father. While

he was some distance down the road, his father saw him and was moved to tears. He ran to him and hugged him and kissed him and kissed him.

"The boy said, 'Dad, I've sinned against God and you, and I'm not fit to be your son any more. . . .' But the father said to his servants, 'You all run quick and get the best suit you can find and put it on him. Get his family ring for his hand and some dress shoes for his feet. Then I want you to bring that stall-fed steer and butcher it, and let's all eat and whoop it up, because this son of mine was given up for dead, and he's still alive; he was lost and is now found.' And they began to whoop it up.

"But his older son was out in the field. When he came in and got almost home, he heard the music and the dancing, and he called one of the little boys and asked him what in the world was going on. The little boy said, 'Why, your brother has come home, and your daddy has butchered the stall-fed steer, because he got him back safe and sound.' At this he blew his top, and wouldn't go in. His father went out and pleaded with him. But he answered his father, 'Look here, all these years I've slaved for you, and never once went contrary to your orders. And yet, at no time have you ever given me so much as a baby goat with which to pitch a party for my friends. But when this son of yours — who has squandered the business on whores — comes home, you butcher for him the stall-fed steer.' But he said to him, 'My boy, my dear boy, you are with me all the time, and what's mine is yours. But I just can't *help* getting happy and whooping it up, because *this brother of yours* was dead and is alive; he was lost and has been found.' " Luke 15:11-32.

In those days, a young son could ask for his share of the inheritance before his father died. And this was not an unusual kind of thing. If the boy wanted to take his money and go off to school, he could do it, or if he wanted to take his bit of money and set himself up in business, he was not making an unusual or unique request of his father. This was his privilege. But if he asked for this division of the estate, then he had no more legal claim. He could not come back later and say, "Well, how 'bout taking me back in?" It was a cutting of the ties, once and for all.

So, this young fellow went into a far country and there he wasted his inheritance living like a fool. And when he came to his senses, he returned home, and his daddy saw him a long ways off and welcomed him back into the family.

Now the older boy was out on the back forty when all this was going on. He was plowing the cotton and the peanuts with his old mule. The day had been hot and the sun was beating down on him. And the mule had been slow and the gnats and horseflies were about to wear him out. He was having it rough, and he's beginning to think very seriously about a call to the ministry. Down our way, they have a saying: "A slow mule and a hot sun have called many a man into the ministry."

So this older son decides to call it a day. And coming in from the fields he sees the house all lit up. And he sees one of the barn boys standing outside.

"Hey, what's going on in there? What's all the lights on for? What's all the music?"

And the little boy says, "Ain't you heard? Where have you been all day? Your brother's come home."

"My what?"

"Your brother!"

"I ain't got no brother. He's dead."

"No, your daddy said he was dead but now he's alive. He's come home."

"Yeah, and I'll bet Pa took him out to the woodshed and. . . ."

"No. He said, 'Go get a suit for him and a ring. Put some shoes on his feet. And get the fatted calf and barbecue it.' "

"Pa said that?"

"Yeah."

"After he'd already given him half the estate, he goes and gives him all that too?"

"Yeah. That's what he did."

And the old boy goes into the barn, puts his mule in, kicks him in the belly, sits down on a big ol' bale of hay, and starts to pout. His daddy goes out there and says, "Son, come on in here and get your plate of barbecue."

"I ain't gonna eat no barbecue."

"What's your trouble?"

"Listen here, Pa. All these years I've been here, I've been a perfect son of yours. If you said, 'Plow peanuts,' I plowed peanuts. If you said, 'Chop cotton,' I chopped cotton. I went with you to church. I got a badge for ten years of perfect attendance, and I've been a good boy here, and I just don't understand how it could be when this, your son, comes home, having wasted your money, after living with harlots, you kill for him the fat calf."

Now where did all this business about harlots come in? Nobody up to this point said anything about harlots. It just said that this younger boy had wasted his money living like a fool; it didn't mean he was running around with women, necessarily.

But this older boy thought that his brother was doing what he would have been doing, if he had been out on his own. He just gave himself away. By judging his brother, he passed judgment on himself. Here is the real prodigal, the one who stayed at home. He was wasting his substance living with those harlots mentally. Everytime he went down the peanut row he was thinking about one of them.

The father reminds him, "Everything I have is yours. But," the father adds, "when this, your brother, comes home, I cannot help but rejoice. For he was lost and he's found; he was dead, and he's alive."

How does this parable end? Did the elder brother come in? Did he say, "I see your point, Dad. Maybe my brother left because I'd been such a hard fellow to get along with. Maybe we ought to give him another chance. I'm glad you treated him like you did. I'm going to go in. I'll join in the dancing, in the music, in the barbecue. I'm glad he came home." Or did the older boy stay outside?

Jesus asks His listeners to write the conclusion. For this "older boy" was standing *right in front of Him as He was telling parables. The religious establishment, the ministers, the church members, and Sunday school teachers who had brought up the issue of the outcasts in the first place, they themselves were the real prodigals.*

These three stories have been instrumental in teaching us that God is interested in the "lost." But our shortsightedness emerges when we make two unwarranted conclusions: (1) Everyone is, after all, lost, and (2) membership in God's family is, therefore, automatic.

Of course, in an ultimate sense, everyone is lost, and those who think themselves to be secure in the kingdom are perhaps most lost of all. But this obscures a critical judgment that Jesus makes. Jesus is not talking about the lost in an ultimate sense. He is talking about a God who discriminates between those who are clearly branded by society as lost and those whom society considers to be healthy and in no need of a physician. [3] People who are "well" and "found" in an everyday existential sense do exist, and the parables of the sheep and coin imply that they may exist in our civilization in numbers that far exceed the presence of the "sick" and "lost." God is not pictured here as a God of love, but as a God of *discriminating* love. We must take this idea seriously and not try to neutralize it by searching for other passages that appear to repudiate it. We must not "systematize"

57

this truth out of existence. There are ninety-nine sheep which God does not rejoice over, nine coins which she takes for granted, [4] and one son who is somewhat justifiably offended at being overlooked. The elder brother speaks on behalf of a majority of the sheep and coins when he protests against the father's unfairness. Perhaps he speaks for us also.

Jesus delivered an inaugural sermon in His hometown of Nazareth that gained Him applause at first — until the people understood what He was saying! Then they tried to throw Him over the nearest cliff. [5] He began by quoting the familiar prophecy about God's mission being aimed at the poor people, the oppressed, the blind, and the downtrodden. Everybody said, "Amen!" Then Jesus made the mistake of turning the message around, so as to put it in sharper focus. He couldn't have put His foot more firmly in His mouth if He had gotten up to address a middle-class congregation and said, "God doesn't care about this church." [6]

The punch of these "lost" parables comes when we turn them around. They are Trojan horse parables. Jesus wasn't about to take the same approach that He took before the hometown folks. But He wanted to make the very same point to these "white church people" and "Sunday school teachers" that came asking why He spent so much time with outcasts. He wanted to show them that they were the real outcasts — the prodigals who stayed home. So He lit a stick of dynamite, covered it over with an interesting story, and presented it to them. By the time these "good" people got these parables unwrapped, He and His disciples were a few miles down the road. Chances are they were still able to hear the explosion. No wonder the "bishops and theologians and key leaders" tried to do away with Him. [7]

5

GOD AGAINST THE RICH!

One of our most sacred beliefs is that God is the God of the church, first of all. But thus far the parables have made us wonder whether a vast number of church members may not be so swollen with religious pride as to be excluded by the narrow door of the kingdom.

And what about the rich? The salvation of the rich is assumed almost as easily as the salvation of the church. The Old Testament has conditioned our understanding to the extent that Proverbs 10:22 is taken by some, at least implicitly, to be the essence of the biblical position: "Riches are a sign of God's blessing." But the parables give us a different view of the wealthy and of what their lives represent. The first insight that the parables provide is that people don't possess wealth so much as wealth possesses people. Clarence offers this translation and commentary regarding Luke 12:13-21.

One day when a big crowd of people were following Jesus someone shouted, "Hey, mis-

ter, how about making my brother divide up the inheritance with me." Jesus turned to him and said, "Say, fellow, has anyone appointed me to be umpire over your financial squabbles?" Then He said to the crowd, "You all really stay on your guard and watch out for all kinds of greediness, because just being rich can't make a man out of you."

Then He told them a story that today may have gone something like this:

The fields of a certain rich man produced abundantly. We don't know the name of this man, so we'll just call him Sam — some of us might even want to call him "Uncle."

Uncle Sam's fields produced an abundance of corn, cotton, peanuts, and soybeans. He had been working on these fields for a long time. He bought them when he and his wife were young. They had worked hard. Many a time they had gone out at the crack of day to do the chores. They spent long days plowing, hoeing cotton, trying to make a big crop so as to pay off the mortgage, buy furniture, get a new car, and put the kids through school. Sometimes they even found time to go to church on Sunday.

There were times at the close of the day when he and his wife would walk out on the hill back of the house and watch the sun paint its beautiful farewell to the day. They would stand there silently and watch it, and sometimes she would hold his hand and say, "It's pretty, ain't it?" And he would say, "It's pretty, Honey, sure is. It's real pretty."

He even found time to hunt arrowheads with his kids, to stalk with them the elusive whippoorwill; and there were times when he would gather them on his lap and read to them from Winnie the Pooh.

As time went on these occasions became rarer. The county agent was there to talk with him about liming his land, contouring, strip farming, soil-building legumes, and all that kind of stuff to make his farm more productive. And there was the stream of machinery salesmen besieging him with all kinds of labor-saving and profit-making equipment.

Increasingly, Uncle Sam became more like the machines that dominated his life. He had little feeling any more, but what did it matter? He was more productive and, better than that, he was making more profit. Long ago his little corncribs had given way to row on row of steel grain bins; his barns now were bulging warehouses. His problem now was not how to make it, but where to store it. True, he had heard that there were people in other lands who were starving, but it was their own fault. They were lazy, ignorant, shiftless, and undeserving. They hadn't mucked and grubbed and scraped like he had; they didn't deserve any better. No sir, no indeed, he wouldn't share his hard-earned goods with them folks. Grain, you know, must be kept in steel bins, not in hungry bellies.

Then one day he looked over his auditor's report and income tax returns. He was quite pleased with the way things were going. He said to himself, "Sam, you old codger, you have enough to live it up for the rest of your life. Put your land in the soil bank, man, get a government loan on your grain, and then, boy, head for Florida. Sam, you're going to recline, dine, wine, and shine."

Then God said to him, "You NITWIT! On this very night all these things are possessing your soul. You don't own them; they own you. And all this stuff you have piled up, whose is it really?" So the poor, rich farmer was struck with the realization that he would continue for the rest of his life in bondage to the things that had enslaved him all along.

"And that's the way it is," said Jesus, "with a man who sets his heart on money and not on God!" [1]

The point being made is that this farmer's *riches* are crying out for his soul. The traditional interpretation is that the man is going to die. Fate or God or some unnamed force is demanding his soul, saying that his time is up. But the Greek text does not say, "This night your soul is being demanded of you." It says, "This night *they* require thy soul of thee" — "they" referring to the "many good things" which the farmer thought *he* owned. These things are telling the farmer what to do so that he can't do that which is desired by God, to whom the "soul" rightfully belongs. This parable is about becoming a slave of money — an appropriate thought in our own credit-card civilization. What we supposedly possess, often on credit, dictates what we must do to secure and maintain it.

Jesus introduces another parable which tells us what it is that wealth demands when it cries out for our souls. The "soul" is a general term that refers to the force that drives us, that motivates and consumes our lives. What is the effect of this force within us? What are the results when our riches start giving us orders, as they inevitably do? Jesus gives us a picture of what happens:

Once there was a rich man, and he put on his tux and stiff shirt, and staged a big affair every day. And there was laid at his gate a poor guy by the name of Lazarus, full of sores, and so hungry he wanted to fill up on the rich man's table scraps. On top of this, the dogs came and licked his sores.

It so happened that the poor fellow died, and the angels seated him at the table with Abraham. The rich man died, too, and was buried. And in the hereafter, the rich man, in great agony, looked up and saw from afar Abraham, and Lazarus sitting beside him at the table. So he shouted to him, "Mr. Abraham, please take pity on me and send Lazarus to dip the end of his finger in some water and rub it over my tongue, because I'm scorching in this heat."

Abraham replied, "Boy, you remember that while you were alive you got the good things (the good jobs, schools, streets, houses, etc.), while at the same time Lazarus got the leftovers. But now, here *he's* got it made, and you're scorching. And on top of all this, somebody has dug a yawning chasm between us and you, so that people trying to get through from here to you can't make it, neither can they get through from there to us."

The rich man said, "Well, then, Mr. Abraham, will you please send him to my father's house, for I have five brothers; let him thoroughly warn them so they won't come to this hellish condition."

Then Abraham said, "They've got the Bible and the preachers; let them listen to them."

But he said, "No, they won't do that, Mr. Abraham. But if somebody will go to them from the dead, they'll change their ways!"

He replied, "Well, if they won't listen to the Bible and the preachers, they won't be persuaded even if someone does get up from the dead." Luke 16:19-31.

This is another one of those Trojan horse episodes in which Jesus conceals His truth. It's a story — it isn't intended to be history. It is not intended to give us a glimpse into the afterlife. It has but one purpose, and that is to portray a truth.

Jesus said, "There was a certain rich man and he was dressed up in a tuxedo and a white shirt and pitched a big party every day, complete with mint juleps and magnolia blossoms. He had it made! There was also a beggar by the name of Lazarus sitting at his gate, full of sores. And he would have been happy to eat the scraps from the table of the rich man. More than that, the dogs came and licked his sores."

This parable contains a play on words in the original text. The word for "beggar" is related to the word for "spit" in Greek. Lazarus was a "spit-upon one," held in contempt by the rich man.

In Jesus's day one of the most contemptible things you could do to a man was to spit in his face. Still isn't too polite. It was out of contempt Jesus was playing on this spittle word. This old rich man, dressed up in a tuxedo, holding a conference, inviting all of his wealthy friends, putting on a big banquet. And poor old Lazarus, lying out there with the sores. And the rich man spit on him. But what did the dogs do? How did they use their spit? They licked his sores. Spittle was thought not only to show contempt, but to have healing properties. Jesus healed a man who was born blind by spitting on the ground, making a salve, and touching the man's eyes. Here, spittle was thought to be something beneficial. The rich man was using his spittle to show contempt. How were the dogs using theirs? To heal. In other words, the dogs were acting in a more human way than a human was.

Most people in Jesus' day would catch the symbolism of these dogs. The dogs — the unsaved people, the unchurched people, the Gentiles, the outcast — they were using their spittle to heal a man. Who was the rich man? He was the person of God's inheritance. He had the law, the prophets, and the writings. He was rich in the sense of his religious heritage. He thought he had an edge on all of God's goodness.

It so happened that the spit-on man died,

and he was carried away by angels to the bosom of Abraham. Jesus had to shift scenery to get over there on the other side of the grave so He could finish His story. Otherwise, His hearers would have been so immediately threatened by truth that they'd have lynched Him on the spot. Jesus will bring the parable back on this side of the grave as soon as He gets to a point where it's safe to do so. In the meantime, everyone has relaxed into thinking that Jesus doesn't have any more to say about the here and now.

The beggar was carried away into the bosom of Abraham. This was Jesus' way of saying that history has a habit of reversing itself. The first shall be last and the last shall be first. The poor beggar was turned upside down. He used to be on the bottom getting scraps from the table. Now he's sitting at the table with the Daddy of the Hebrew race. Lazarus is sitting right next to Abraham. That was a high honor for any Jew, especially one that was full of sores.

Where is the rich man? He is in torment. And he sees Abraham from afar and Lazarus at his bosom. He shouts out, "Oh, Father Abraham, send me my water boy. Water boy! Quick! I'm just about to perish down here. I need a drink of water." That old rich guy had always hollered for his water boy: "Boy, bring me water! Boy, bring me this! Boy, bring me that! Get away, boy! Come here, boy!"

But Abraham throws it right back in his teeth. Abraham says to him, "Boy!" Ain't that somethin'? Abraham slings it back to him

for the first time and says, "Boy, you remember that you got the good things while you
were alive and Lazarus got what was left.
You got the good schools. Lazarus got what
was left. You got the good sections of town
and the paved streets. Lazarus got what was
left. You got the good churches. Lazarus got
what was left. You remember that, don't you?
Don't you remember that? Back there when
you were alive, before you died? You got the
good things. Lazarus got the crumbs that had
fallen from your table. Don't you remember
that?"

"Hmmm. Seems like I do have a few mem-
ories."

"You betcha. Now Lazarus is the guest of
honor and you are in great pain. And, more
than that, there is between us and you a
yawning chasm so that those who want to go
between can't make it."

This is really the cutting edge of the parable, this yawning chasm. It's broken up traffic. The bridge is blasted. Big chasm between
'em. We can't get to you. You can't get to us.
Who dug that ditch? Who dug that chasm?
Where did it come from? That rich man knows
who dug it. HE DUG IT! And why did he dig
it? He dug it to break up traffic. He dug it to
keep guys with sores out. He didn't want the
value of his property to go down when sore
people moved into his neighborhood. You know,
you'd better be careful how you dig ditches
to keep people out; you might want to cross
them yourself some day. Be careful when you

blow up bridges. You might want to cross that bridge some day. This rich man is caught in his own trap.

Then he says, "Well, sir, Father, I beg you to send him to my family, for I have five brothers. Let him testify to them, lest they come to the same place of torment that I have come to. I've got five brothers thinking just like I am. They're digging ditches, they're breaking up traffic, they're erecting barriers around themselves. Oh, Father Abraham, I know what a horrible thing this is now. Please let this Lazarus go back and tell my brothers what an awful thing it is to dig chasms."

And ol' Father Abraham says, "They got Moses and the prophets. Let them listen to them." In other words, he's saying, "They got the Bible and the preachers. What's the matter with those guys? Can't they read? Can't they hear? They got preachers all over everywhere who have skill in the interpretation of the Scriptures. Let them listen to what the Scriptures are saying."

"Oh, Father Abraham, they don't listen to those preachers. I know. I sat under preachers for thirty years and never paid attention to a single thing they said. But you just let Lazarus go down there — let him just ooze through the room a few times. I think you'll get some results. But they ain't goin' to listen to the preachers. And they ain't goin' to listen to the Bible."

Abraham said, "Oh, no, if they won't listen to the Bible and the preachers, they won't be persuaded if someone goes to them from the dead. If you can't get results by appealing to their minds and hearts, you're not going to get results by scaring them into the kingdom. You can't populate heaven with refugees from hell."

So this parable is a beautiful dramatization of the fact that the last shall be first and the first shall be last. And any time you break up traffic, you're blowing the bridges that some day you might want to travel.

We are all accustomed to living with gulfs that keep us from each other: the gulf of wealth, the gulf of pride, the gulf of race, the gulf of sex. Perhaps we would not admit we dug these ditches to keep certain people out. We just worked hard and got wealthy, and it's not our fault if poor people can't afford to live in our neighborhood, belong to our clubs, or join our church. The point of this parable that really condemns us is not that we dug the ditch. To a certain extent, if you were born white, if you were born American, and if your family could afford to "civilize" and educate you, then maybe fate did have a hand in digging the ditch. The question is, What are you and I doing, while we still have time, to fill in that ditch and to overcome the boundaries that shut other people in or out of our fellowship?

Building bridges must become our priority. We can no longer get by with the claim that we are open to anyone who *comes to us. We've got to go to them.* We can't salve our consciences by inviting and "helping" people to become rich along with us. We've got to become poor along with them. The burden of action — of bridge-building — is upon us. We must find ways to dispossess ourselves of whatever separates us from the least of our international brothers and sisters.

We must cross over into their world out of compassion for the beggars who sit at our gates. Our own dispossession will go part of the way toward healing the sores of humanity. But, more importantly, we must dispossess ourselves for our own sakes. This is the punch that the parables deliver most decisively. *We* are the victims of the barriers that we have erected with the help of fate, circumstance, and the "natural thing to do." We have shut ourselves out of the family of the Father because we have failed to realize that "those who are on the top will be on the bottom," and that at this very moment our goods are demanding, and receiving, our souls. And that is why God cannot be God of the rich.

The United States represents 6 percent of the world's population and 60 percent of the world's wealth. To say that God can't be God of the rich is, therefore, the same as to say that God can't be God of middle-class America. Our wealth/poverty is not measured by the amount of money we owe on cars, appliances, and homes compared to the amount of money we have in the bank. Practically all of us could plead poverty if that were the standard. It is measured, instead, by the outward comfort of our lives compared to the misery of the masses who are ill-fed, ill-clothed, and ill-housed. And by this standard all of us must confess wealth. *The gulf between ourselves and the poor is the gulf between ourselves and God.*

6

DISTURBING THE PEACE

Two sure signs of culture are amiability and restraint. These virtues carry us a long way into the good graces of civilized society. In our better homes and schools and churches we have been taught diplomacy, courtesy, and serenity. If cleanliness is indeed next to godliness, composure cannot be far removed.

Imagine our surprise, then, when we discover that smooth, cool civility is sufficient to *disqualify* us from participation in the God Movement. God is not the spiritual Father of us all. He is the Father of the distraught and the impetuous who reach out in desperation for an answer to injustice.

Desperation is so alien to most of us. Can the parables sober us and help us to recover the foolhardiness that must characterize our citizenship in the kingdom? Is there any recklessness that we can muster, or have we become too civilized for membership in God's family? Have we made ourselves at home with the "peace" of this world? Have we placed sufficient geographical and emotional distance between ourselves and the world's starving, lonely masses?

The biblical imagery of hungering and thirsting after justice conveys an intensity that we often lack. Hungering and thirsting call forth the necessity for daring action. To avoid the need for such action, God structured the ideal Hebrew culture so that both neighbors and government officials would be unfailing in their supply of justice. They represented, at their best, the normative personal and institutional response to the nature of God and to the plight of the oppressed.

> Yahweh your God is God of gods and Lord of lords, the great God, triumphant and terrible, never partial, never to be bribed. It is he who sees justice done for the orphan and the widow, who loves the stranger and gives him food and clothing. Deuteronomy 10:17-18, *Jerusalem Bible*.

Orphans, widows, and strangers are the oppressed — those for whom God especially [1] cares. For any civilization to disenfranchise these people, for any world order to overlook the legitimate needs of its third world brothers and sisters — those who are strangers to food and clothing — is for that civilization to forfeit its own right to exist. [2] God has been merciful to us, who were once strangers to Him. Therefore, the imperative for us is transformed from a mandate for mercy to a mandate for simple justice. As a matter of fairness, we are to reflect the goodness that has been shown to us.

74

In fact, we have received such an undeserved abundance that whatever we might give to others, even if we were to deliver our bodies as living sacrifices, would only amount to what was reasonable and right. The following passage demonstrates this new, radical, liberating perspective that we are to have on life.

Then Rock[3] sidled up and asked, "Sir, how often should I forgive my brother when he keeps doing me wrong? Seven times?"

"I wouldn't say seven times," Jesus replied, "but *seventy times seven*! That's why the God Movement is like a big businessman who wanted to settle the accounts of his customers. As he started to do so, one customer came in who owed a bill of more than ten thousand dollars. He had nothing to pay on the account, so the businessman told the sheriff to put up for sale everything the guy had and apply it to the debt. But the fellow did a song and dance. 'Please give me more time and I'll pay every cent!' he begged. The businessman was touched by the guy's pitiful pleas, so he let him go and marked off the debt. Then that same guy went out and found a man who owed him a hundred dollars. Grabbing him around the neck, he choked him and said, 'Pay me that money you owe.'

'Please give me a little more time,' the man begged, 'and I'll pay every cent.' But he refused and, instead, he swore out a warrant for him. When the little man's friends found out about it, they were really upset, so they went and told the big businessman all that had happened. Then the big businessman sent for the guy who had owed him the huge debt and said to him, 'You

75

lowdown bum! I marked off all that debt for you because you begged me to. Shouldn't you, then, have been kind to that little man just as I was kind to you?' Still hot under the collar, he turned the fellow over to the law to be thrown into the clink until every last dime of the debt had been paid. And my spiritual Father will treat you along the same lines unless every single one of you forgives your brother from your heart." Matthew 18:21-35.

For those of us who have received God's forgiveness, there is no longer any possibility that we can withhold forgiveness from others. Forgiving others is now a matter of justice, of fairness, of loving others as we ourselves have been loved. Likewise, meeting the needs of others in regard to the necessities of life is no longer a matter of mercy, although the needy may be begging us for "mercy" from their perspective. But from our perspective, standing as we do in the place of blessing, enjoying the "seventy times seven" relationship to God, how hypocritical it would be to take Rock's suggestion seriously and stop at seven in our relationship to those who beg from us. We must be mature as our heavenly Father is mature.

Rock throught that forgiving seven times would be mercy enough. Jesus countered that seven times is not only a shortage of mercy, it isn't even sufficient to fulfill the minimum daily requirements of justice!

Jesus draws us two pictures of society that are not very complimentary. Justice has fallen upon hard days. The sources of justice (in these two instances they are, appropriately, a neighbor and a judge) have grown callous.

When we look at the first picture, the parable of the neighbor at midnight, we should remember that the provision of bread for the stranger was a matter of justice within the Hebrew culture. It was not optional. It was not "merciful."

If a stranger lives with you in your land . . . you must count him as one of your own countrymen and love him as yourself. Leviticus 19:33-34, *Jerusalem Bible*.

So the following is a parable of the struggle for justice.

Suppose you have a friend who comes to you in the middle of the night and says, "Hey, neighbor, how about lending me three loaves of bread. A friend of mine has just arrived at my house, and I don't have anything to serve him." Then you'll call out from inside the house, "Please don't disturb me! I've already locked the door and have got all the kids to sleep. I can't get up and let you have anything." I really believe that even though you won't get up and let him have something out of friendship for him, you will crawl out and let him have whatever he needs if he keeps yelling and pounding on the door.

So that's why I'm telling you, start asking and it will be given to you; start looking, and you will find; start knocking, and it will be opened to you. For every asker receives, every seeker finds, and to every one who knocks the door is opened. Luke 11:5-10 [4]

Jesus is saying that we are in a sad state of affairs if it takes "yelling and pounding" to bring justice. The Greek word for "yelling and pounding" refers to the man's impudence. This man, making such a racket in the middle of the night, is shamelessly disturbing the peace. The demand for justice overrides the demand for civility, for proper procedures, for "wait until morning." The time for justice is now, so we should be quick to "start asking," "start looking," and "start knocking." The Greek verbs indicate a continuous action, as is consistent with the parable. We are to "start asking" and keep on asking. We are to yell and pound until the door is opened.

To the extent that we possess the world's goods, we should see ourselves as the sleepy and reluctant neighbor in the parable. We should be ashamed, in this case, that it takes so much clamor to get us to respond to basic human need. Does the third world have to break down the door of the church to get it to react? Does James Foreman have to disrupt a worship service, no less, and issue a "Black Manifesto"? Whether he does or not is up to us. How soundly asleep are we? And how much do we have in the way of rationalization and red tape to perpetuate injustice?

But suppose God is the one who is asleep at midnight. As was pointed out in the Deuteronomy passage, He is the One who ultimately "sees justice done . . . who loves the stranger and gives food and clothing." And Luke properly implies in the verses that follow this parable that the ultimate appeal for justice is to God Himself. If *we* know how to give good gifts to our children, even though we are sinful and our children have to be a little persistent sometimes to get our attention, how much more readily will *God* respond to even our most casual request? He is certainly not "asleep," nor is He callous to the pursuit of justice. So Luke infers that if it were up to God alone, justice would be done swiftly. By the time the needy one was ready to knock, God would be waiting at the door with the necessary food. The catch is that *in this world, at this time, it is not up to God alone*. If it were, this parable would be meaningless. God has chosen to act through His people. This is not primarily a parable about who God is, but about whom we must be. We must be light sleepers. We must not wait for violence to be done before we do justice for the needy at our gate.

Suppose our traveling friend comes to us and we act on behalf of God as we should. We take him in, even though he is an unexpected guest. But we discover that we "don't have anything to serve him." The requirements of justice are beyond our immediate control. We, along with our third world friends, all become strangers to bread. What shall we strangers do?

In an ultimate sense, we go to God, of course. But in this case God's ordained representative, assuming that our appeals to our Christian brothers and sisters have been exhausted, is the state. [5] The state is to be, in many situations, the immediate and perhaps the only possible source of human justice, and now we must resort to these resources of government. We must not only be light sleepers when the friend comes to our house, but we must be loud knockers when we appeal to our neighbors on our friend's behalf. The cupboards of the church are bare. The church itself is needy. The church doesn't ask the state for resources it already possesses. We don't take our friend next door if we ourselves can feed him. We don't expect the institutions of government to respond with a compassion that we ourselves don't possess. Our friend has come to us; we are awake and active on his behalf; but we are powerless. Surely we will not stop knocking just because the door of the church cannot (or will not) open to us.

We will go to where the power is. This parable indicates that even though we ourselves are oppressed, we still have the responsibility to go "next door" and appeal to the institutions of government to fulfill the purpose for which they were ordained. The state now plays the role of the sleepy and reluctant neighbor. Shall we be timid lest we arouse this threatening giant and incur its wrath? Or shall we create such a nonviolent ruckus that the state will give in to our demands just to be rid of us? [6] If Jesus has indeed come to cast fire upon the earth, it will not be kindled

80

by modest and polite women and men. The God Movement is not made up of such stuff.

God is anxious that we cultivate within us this bright aspect of discipleship that our society has taught us to suppress. We live in a cruel world. We cannot be meek and mild on behalf of our friends. There comes a time when we must rise up with all the conviction that is in us and shatter the rationalized, pragmatic procedures that typify our society. We want bread for our friends. We will not wait until morning. We will not cool our compassion or our tempers. We will not listen to "reason." We will not go through "proper" channels. And we will disrupt and disturb the slumber and the apathy of our culture until justice is served.

This impudence is part of the bright side of discipleship because it is part of the nature of God.

Yahweh advances like a hero,
his fury is stirred like a warrior's.
He gives the war shout, raises the hue and cry,
marches valiantly against his foes.

"From the beginning I have been silent,
I have kept quiet, held myself in check.
I groan like a woman in labor,
I suffocate, I stifle.

"I will turn mountain and hill to desert,
wither all their greenery,
turn rivers to pools
and dry up lakes.

81

"But I will make the blind walk along the road
and lead them along paths.
I will turn darkness into light before them
and rocky places into level tracks.

"These things I will do,
and not leave them undone." Isaiah 42:13-16,
  Jerusalem Bible.

This Old Testament passage is written in the context of a chapter about the servant of Yahweh who brings true justice. One can almost see the Messiah yelling and pounding at the bar of justice and overturning the tables of the money-changers at the Temple. If our enlightened society calls this behavior "ugly," we must remember that God has a different notion of beauty. Perhaps the measured wisdom of our culture is itself ugly and oppressive.

A companion parable which develops this same idea of the relationship of the Christian and the state is found in Luke 18. In this second drama there is no doubt that the government, not God or the church, needs to be aroused from its bed of judicial apathy. Jesus is careful to point out that the judge in this story admits to not even a basic regard for God, and therefore he cannot represent the church.

One time in a certain city there was a judge who didn't believe in God, and didn't give a hoot about people. In the same city was a widow, and she came to him repeatedly and said, "Please, hear my case against so-and-so." He put her off for a long time, but finally he said to himself: "Even though I don't believe in God and don't give a hoot for people, yet because this woman has got it in for me, I'll hear her case before she finally nags me to death." Luke 18:2-5.

The word translated "nags" is a graphic word in the Greek with a violent physical connotation. The verb form literally means "to beat black and blue." Perhaps this widow brought her cane to the courthouse! In any case, we have an intensification of the impudence we discovered in Luke 11.

There are times when causing trouble is the witness we must raise for the sake of justice. There are times when the depth of our concern for something will cause us to overstep the bounds of a common law and order for the sake of a higher law and order. I do not believe that Jesus wants us to *literally* bruise the body politic, but Jesus uses strong language to make His point: what is just in God's eyes is more important than standard operating procedure in the eyes of our culture. If we are to reflect the intensity of God's compassion for the victims of oppression, we must rise above the requirements of "good citizenship."

Justice and mercy are often seen in Scripture as the fruit of Christian commitment. God requires these instead of rituals and churchmanship. [7] Any culture that has received the light of the gospel is under a tremendous obligation to order its national life according to

God's law. Israel failed at the time of Jesus. And the United States, which presumes to say that it is "one nation under God," has also failed. Indeed, the entire Western world is mocked by its steeples and creeds. We have received God's grace, but we have not returned the fruit of obedience. And this is why God is prepared to rescind His grace from the enlightened and "religious" and give it to the outsiders, the third world, the "pagans."

This story of God's action is recorded in a parable in Matthew 21.

"Once there was a farmer who set out a peach orchard, built a fence around it, bought some equipment, and put up a packing shed. Then he rented it to some sharecroppers and left. When peach-picking time came, he sent his workers to the croppers to get his share of the fruit. But the croppers took his workers and beat one of them, killed another, and stoned the other. So he tried again, this time sending more important workers than before, but the croppers treated them the same way. Finally he sent his son, thinking that surely they would respect *him*. But when the croppers saw the son they got together and said, 'Hey, there's the old man's boy. Let's kill this cat and take over his estate!' So they grabbed him and dragged him out of the orchard and murdered him. Now, when the owner of the orchard comes, what will he do to those croppers?"

They answered, "Why, he'll tear those bastards to bits, and let out the orchard to croppers who'll give him his share of the fruit at harvesttime."

84

Jesus asked them, "Haven't you ever read in the Bible: 'The stone which the craftsmen rejected was selected as the cornerstone. This was done by the owner, and is an amazing sight for us.'? Now that's why I'm telling you that the God Movement will be taken out of your hands and turned over to people who will be productive. . . ." The ministers and church people listened to his Comparisons, and were aware that they were aimed at them. They were dying to arrest him, but feared the crowd, who regarded him as a man of God. Matthew 21:33-46.

The landowner in this parable had fixed up a plot of land. And he leased it out to some sharecroppers and went away to spend the winter in Florida. He was going to retire, because he was tired of fooling with the farming himself. He was going to come back from time to time to get his share of the fruit.

The parable is directed to the nation Israel. Jesus said to Israel, "God leased you this land. He entered into a contract or covenant with you in good faith, expecting you to carry out your end of the bargain. He sent His servants to you. These were the prophets. And what did you do with them?"

"Well, we took up an offering and gave them an honorarium."

No, that's not what they did with them. Back in those days, a prophet didn't have any better sense than to preach a sermon that the people could understand. And they got the point. And the prophet got the point too, along with a few rocks.

"Well," God said, "I'll send them more and try again." So He sent them Isaiah, Amos, Micah, Obadiah, and Malachi. But they took them out and beat them, too. "Oh," God thought, "what kind of folks did I rent My orchard to? What am I going to do? Oh, I know. I'm going to ask My Boy to go up there. He will carry My authority with Him, and surely when they see Him, they will have respect for Him. I'm gonna send Him." And God so loved the world that He gave His only Son. He came to His own, and His own received Him not. They took Him out of the orchard, out on the little hillside, and there they lynched Him.

"What do you think is going to happen to those farmers?" Jesus asked. The church people and ministers who had been listening said, "We know what'll happen to 'em. The land will be taken away and be given to somebody who'll act right."

Now, this isn't the judgment of God's severity being handed down on people. It is the judgment of history itself upon nations that do not bring forth the fruit.

This was one of Jesus' parables where the religious people of His day got the point immediately, despite the Trojan horse technique. Hopefully we can also get the point that Jesus is making about us proper Christian citizens. God has leased out His orchard to us, and we have at best returned a diluted "faith." We have substituted "worship" for obedience and practicality for reckless faithfulness. Reasonable men and women acting judiciously crucified Jesus, and our civil religion ratifies the verdict. We are the children of propriety, and that is why God is in the market for some new farming partners. The broad heavily-traveled path of civilized behavior is not an adequate response to nor reflection of the nature of God.

When I was a teenager in Pittsburgh with access to the family car, my father would often help me by giving directions to various destinations. Dad was a traveling salesman who knew his way around the city. But even for him Pittsburgh presented problems with its hills, rivers, tunnels, and triangles. Out of hundreds of streets no two seemed to run parallel. After struggling with a road map and his memory for a while, Dad would often shrug his shoulders and comment, "You can't get there from here."

And that's the way it is with the kingdom of God. If we are going to stand fast with reason and practicality, law and order, as the highest good; if we are enslaved by the traditional road maps that others pass down to us; if we are thoroughgoing children of our culture, then we can't get there from here. When you're sitting in a crowded auditorium and you smell smoke, you've got to disturb the peace a little as a matter of justice.

CHILDREN OF ARROGANCE

Whose children are we? We are children of the church, of mammon, and of culture. And these parents have cost us our humility (we see ourselves as "good" people), our vulnerability (we have dug a ditch around our lives to keep away the needy), and our impetuous zeal for the kingdom (we are quite at peace with *this* world, thank you).

We never made the decision to leave the kingdom. We never consciously became God's enemies. And this is what troubles us. We don't hate Jesus! So why are we cast in the role of outside adversaries? We look, feel, and sound like Christians. Yet the parables have made us out to be villains.

There is a parable that helps us understand our origins and the anatomy of our silent rebellion.

Then he laid before them another Comparison: "The God Movement is like a man who planted certified seed in his field. Then after everybody had gone to bed, his enemy came and over-planted the wheat with zizania [wild rice]. When it all came up and started to grow, the zizania was clearly present. The farmer's fieldhands came to him and said, 'Sir, didn't you plant certified seed in your field? Then how come it's got zizania in it?' He replied, 'An enemy did that!' The fieldhands asked, 'Do you want us to go and chop it out?' The farmer said, 'No, because you might dig up the wheat with the zizania. Let them both grow until harvesttime. Then I'll say to the harvest workers, "Gather all the zizania first and pile it up for burning, and then harvest the wheat and put it in my barn."

Then he left the crowds and went into the house. His students gathered around him and said, "Please unravel for us the Comparison of the field of zizania." He answered, "The farmer who planted the certified seed is the son of man; the field is the world; the certified seed are the people who do God's will; the zizania are the people who do the will of the evil one; the enemy is the Confuser; the harvest is the fruition of the era; and the harvesters are God's messengers. So, just as the zizania was piled and burned, that's the way it will be at the fruition of the era. The son of man will send out his messengers and they'll collect everything in his Movement that's offensive and all the criminals, and they'll burn them in a roaring furnace. In there, they'll be howling and snapping their teeth. Then the just will shine like the sun in their Father's Movement. Now let *that* percolate through. Matthew 13:24-30, 36-43.

The man in this parable is a real good farmer. He didn't just go buy any kind of seed. He got what had been certified by the State Seed Association as purebred. So he planted certified seed in his field, and while people slept, his enemy came and planted zizania in the midst of the wheat and went away. This is what you call overplanting. You plant your field and then somebody comes along and over-seeds it with zizania. Now zizania was that particularly obnoxious weed that you paid not to have in there. It's a kind of weed that closely resembles wheat. It's difficult to tell it from the real thing. The farmer wisely decides to let the wheat and the zizania grow up together until the time of the harvest, when the wheat will be gathered into the barn and the zizania will be put into bundles to burn.

Now, this was a rather hard parable for Jesus' disciples to crack open. So they came and said to Him, "Will you please bust open that story about the zizania? We just can't get it cracked. Rock hammered at it, busted his hammer handle, and didn't get anywhere. Andy tried it. He busted his finger. And Nathaniel tried it and he busted out with some Hebraic expletives." They were havin' one ol' time tryin' to bust open that parable.

What is this story all about? The common interpretation is that Jesus is talking about the end of the world. When the nations get through arguing and bumping each other's heads there will be one big boom and that will be the end of things and we'll just have fragments left. And the angels will come down here and try to salvage what they can.

But this isn't what Jesus is talking about. He isn't talking about the end of the world in the sense that we think of it. This termination of the age means the end of the old worldly age. The new age is the age of the family of the Father; it's the revolution. As the revolution comes in, the old age is terminated. The end of the world in this respect is taking place all the time. Where the truth is preached and practiced, there is the end of darkness. Wherever freedom comes in, that is the end of the world for slavery. Wherever the kingdom of God, of the Spirit, is preached, there is the end of the world. It doesn't mean the destruction of the world, it means the end of its influence. For instance, I'm quite sure that one of the reasons Koinonia has run into so much difficulty is because we are surrounded by a lot of people who believe that the plantation system has to be maintained in order to preserve a healthy economic life. And they see in the preaching of the gospel of Jesus, and the practicing of it, the end of the plantation system with its exploitation of labor. For them the preaching of the gospel is the end of the world, the end of their world.

Jesus is saying to these religious people who thought that God was going to go on tolerating the wickedness that was in Israel, "Look here, God planted you a long time ago. He sent you preachers and prophets and they have preached to you, but somehow or another they have let the wicked one of the world come in and introduce into your midst

*all kinds of wickedness. God is not going to
tolerate that indefinitely in his kingdom."*

We became enemies of God without our
knowing it. We were planted in secret and
grew up as well-disguised intruders. And we
fooled our neighbors and even ourselves
with our pseudospirituality. But the son of
man knows the unmistakable signs of illegitimacy. We are zizania — imposter children —
and God cannot tolerate us in His kingdom.
The church, mammon, and culture have oper-
ated as sophisticated fronts for the enemy.

If we could give this enemy a name, an
appropriate one would be "Arrogance." In
mythology, it was arrogance that prompted
the angel to claim the place of God and that
led to his subsequent dismissal from the heavenly realm. In the Old Testament, it was
arrogance that characterized the serpent's approach to Eve: "Did God really say. . . ?"
And the serpent planted arrogance within the
human family when he tempted them to "be
like gods." [1]

Now that we are far removed from these in-
cidents we are naive enough to think that we
are immune. In truth we are the victims of
a raging epidemic of pride. It has crept into
our sacred institutions and made them its
breeding ground.

Wealth, religion, and a casual lifestyle are
not the origin of our illegitimacy; they are the
outward signs. They are the milieu in which
pride manifests and reproduces itself. Jesus

gets to the root of the problem in His parables against arrogance.

He gave this Comparison to certain ones who had a high regard for their own goodness, but looked down their noses at others: "Two men went into the chapel to pray. The one was a church member, the other was an unsaved man. The church member stood up and prayed to himself like this: 'O God, I thank you that I'm not like other people — greedy, mean, promiscuous — or even like this unsaved man. *I* go to church *twice* on Sunday, and *I* am a faithful *tither* of all my income.' But the unsaved man, standing way off, wouldn't even lift up his eyes, but knelt down and cried, 'O God, have mercy on a sinner like me.' I'm telling you, this man went home cleaned up rather than that one. For everyone who puts *himself* on a pedestal will be laid low, and everyone who lays himself low will be put on a pedestal." Luke 18:9-14.

Two men went up into the Temple to pray. One was a Pharisee, and he was a nice Pharisee. [2] *He would've qualified as chairman of the board of deacons in any of our churches. He prayed. He was there for midweek prayer meetings every time, which is certainly something. He was a tither, and that's not to be sneered at. And he was a "faster." That meant he really observed all the religious observances. He was there for Easter; he was there for every holiday and every holy day. He was there for the pastor's anniversary; he contributed quite a bit to the fund for the purchase of the new auto-*

mobile. He was an active member of the religious
establishment. In fact, he was so proud of his
record that he was afraid God had lost it. And
so he proceeds to reopen the file so that if
God, perchance, had lost the original, he could
furnish him with a carbon. And he begins
to inform God of just what his qualifications
are; and they are considerable.

On the other hand, there was this old publican. These were people who were about the
equivalent of a fellow traveler. They collab-
orated with the military occupying forces to
collect the taxes from the Jewish people; and
they were about the most despised and unpopu-
lar people. You couldn't have held up a more
despicable person than Jesus did. He lets this
man, the lowest man on the totem pole, go to
the same Temple. Now, he didn't ask God to
open his file; he had to begin with just a very
simple prayer: "O God, have mercy on me, the
sinner."

Now, Jesus raises the question, which of
them got his prayers answered? They
both did; they both got their prayers answered. The old publican asked for forgiveness and that's what he got. The old Pharisee asked for nothing and that's what he
got. Read it. He asked for nothing what-
soever. His was one of these informative
prayers. He just told God what was going
on.

Again the thought returns to haunt us:
"For everyone who puts *himself* on a pedestal

94

will be laid low, and everyone who lays himself low will be put on a pedestal." It is repeated in the parable of the places of honor in Luke 14.

Noting the scramble for the places of honor at the table, he gave some advice to the church leaders who had invited him. "When you are invited by someone to a banquet, don't go immediately to the head table. It might be that some big shot with a higher title than yours has been invited, too, and the person in charge of seating arrangements will have to say to you, 'Please let this gentleman have your seat.' Then with embarrassment you'll begin to step down to the lower seat. But when you're invited, take the most inconspicuous seat, and if the emcee comes in and says to you, 'Hello, my friend. Come on up here,' then you'll feel honored before all the guests. For anyone who promotes himself will be humiliated, and he who humbles himself will be promoted." Luke 14:7-11.

This keynote of pride binds many of the parables together. It accounts for the rampant nationalism of Jesus' time and of our own. "We are the children of Abraham." We're Number One. God strips us naked when He tells us that He can mass-produce children of Abraham out of stones. [3] Pride led the elder brother to promote himself. It tripped the rich farmer into thinking he could "recline, dine, wine, and shine!"

Jesus got into trouble with His friends and

neighbors in Nazareth when He offended their pride. He could have asked them for a million-dollar pledge to underwrite His ministry to the oppressed, and they would have supported Him. But the suggestion that God might leave them behind in His quest for the "outsiders" was sufficient to mobilize an instant lynching party. We all forget that we were once outsiders. We were the original pile of rocks that God brought to life, and if we resist the thought that God could justly return us to the rubble heap, then we are ZIZANIA! We are still outsiders, and our arrogance in thinking that we deserve to be insiders prevents us from accepting God's gracious offer of adoption.

CHILDREN OF GRACE

The parables treated thus far have given us a fresh understanding of the nature of God and a disconcerting picture of discipleship. We have not seen God in the abstract, but in those concrete situations in which His existence touches our own. The parables do not concentrate on God's holiness or eternality. They focus on His fatherhood. His fatherhood touches us when we realize our lostness and our poverty. We show ourselves to be His children when we respond with a consuming zeal for the things of God: justice and compassion.

I have cast the preceding chapters in a strong negative light because the negative point of view was most applicable to Jesus' earliest listeners. Jesus spoke about the lost in Luke 15, but He spoke in response to the comment of the "white church people" and "Sunday school teachers." [1] These people were the ones whom Jesus left behind, the "healthy" who had no need of a physician. The rub came when the good folk realized that God's seeking and waiting for the lost left them alone on the periphery of the kingdom. And that kind of indignity caused many of them to stalk out of the kingdom altogether.

The parables of the rich farmer and the rich man and Lazarus reveal a God, particularly in the latter case, who is concerned for the poor. But their main thrust is against the rich. The parables of the friend asking for bread in the middle of the night and the widow asking for a hearing from the disinterested judge depict a God who rewards those who persistently pursue justice in the midst of an unjust world. But these parables also have a sting: God ignores those who seek His righteous kingdom at a leisurely and civilized pace. This casual attitude is rooted in the arrogance of those who feel that their own high standing within society is proof of their own virtue, society's wisdom, and God's approval.

It is not sufficient for us to summarize these parables by saying that God loves sinners, poor people, and seekers. The punch that absolutely devastates us is that God doesn't seem to care about the righteous, the rich, and the cultured. The people who are most at home in the church are most out of place in the kingdom of God!

Is there any hope then for those of us who stand outside the kingdom as the parables have defined it? Yes. Human nature is subject to change. We must put great emphasis on the fact that was discussed in Chapter Four: the elder son may yet be reunited with his father and his brother.

The last few verses in the parable of the

waiting father, commonly known as the parable of the prodigal son, provide the best example in all of the gospels of Jesus extending an olive branch to the church people of Palestine:

But his older son was out in the field. When he came in and got almost home, he heard the music and the dancing, and he called one of the little boys and asked him what in the world was going on. The little boy said, "Why, your brother has come home, and your daddy has butchered the stall-fed steer, because he got him back safe and sound." At this he blew his top, and wouldn't go in. His father went out and pleaded with him. But he answered his father, "Look here, all these years I've slaved for you, and never once went contrary to your orders. And yet, at no time have you ever given me so much as a baby goat with which to pitch a party for my friends. But when this son of yours — who has squandered the business on whores — comes home, you butcher for him the stall-fed steer." But he said to him, "My boy, my dear boy, you are with me all the time, and what's mine is yours. But I just can't *help* getting happy and whooping it up, because *this brother of yours* was dead and is alive; he was lost and has been found." Luke 15:25-32.

The elder brother represents the righteous people of Jesus' day, the people who, with some justification, could claim that they had dutifully served God over the years without complaint and without going contrary to His orders. These are the people who felt betrayed because Jesus was spending time with outcasts while excluding themselves from His fellowship. Perhaps many of us have the same attitude as this elder brother.

The father does not rebuke his bitter, sulking son, because the son's response is understandable as the immediate reaction of human nature to the situation. But if this elder son had realized that his sonship was of grace, and not the result of twenty-or-so years of devotion, he would have overcome his hurt feelings and joined the party. The mission of the father is to help him go beyond his initial distress. The father "pleads" with him — the Greek word refers to a tender and compassionate appeal. The father calls him "son" — a designation which is not routine, which is best translated by Clarence's phrase: "my boy, my dear boy." When the son hears the words "what's mine is yours," he is receiving a genuine invitation. When we have considered the parables fully, we realize that God does not bar us from the kingdom any more than the father kept his elder son away from the festivities. Only our arrogance can finally lock us out.

Jesus is delivering these hard parables to us not as a last word of utter condemnation, but as a final appeal to us to abandon our elder brother role, our self-assurance, our apathy, our possessiveness, our casual "obedience." We may yet strike a bargain if we truly recognize that our day in court has arrived and found us to be the children of arrogance.

Clarence spoke of Jesus' concern for us in this way:

While he preached love and kindness, and while a number of his parables are spoken in great tenderness, Jesus nevertheless comes at us with great warning — as a man would warn with great urgency a child who was about to step on a rattlesnake. We can see in these parables something of Jesus' great love coupled with a great sense of urgency. As mankind almost puts his foot on the rattler, Jesus leaps at us with a story to warn us of the danger lurking in the grass. These parables, while they might be frightening, can be tremendously profitable, because I have found that if there is a rattlesnake in the grass, even though it makes your hair just stand up on end, the best thing for you is to know where it is. It's the unknown snake that has the power to kill.

The parable that speaks most clearly to our dilemma, and to our hope, is found in Luke 13.

A fellow had a peach tree planted in his orchard, and one day he came looking for some fruit on it but didn't find anything. He said to the hired hand, "Listen here, for three years I've come looking for some fruit on that peach tree and I haven't found a peach. Chop it down. Why let it take up space?" But the hired hand said, "Sir, let it stay just one more year, and I'll hoe around it and put some manure on it. If it should bear fruit then, okay; if it doesn't, chop it down." Luke 13:6-9.

The comparison, or parable, is made between the peach tree and the nation Israel — the nation that thought of itself as the people of God. The story is open-ended. Does the overdose of grace make the tree fruitful, or does the hired hand have to chop it down a year later? Jesus leaves it to us to complete the story. The father who waited for the prodigal son now waits for the elder brother.

Hopefully we have already seen that justice and mercy are only two different ways of viewing the same process. From the standpoint of God, for us to forgive seventy times seven or lay down our lives is only a matter of reasonable justice. From the standpoint of the oppressed, even a few crumbs from our table would be considered undeserved grace. Another parable makes the point more sharply:

> Suppose one of you has a servant chopping cotton or feeding chickens. When he comes to the house that night, would you say to him, "Come on and let's eat"? No, indeed! You would say to him, "Wash up and get supper for me, and wait on me while I'm eating and drinking, and when I get through then you can have your supper." Does one *thank* a servant for merely doing what he is told? All right, that's the way it is with you. When you've done what you've been told, you should say, "We're but undeserving servants doing our duty." Luke 17:7-10 [2]

We're but undeserving servants when we consider what we have received from God:

102

mercy. We're only doing what His grace constrains us to do, justice, when obedience takes us beyond a nine-to-five faithfulness. There is no overtime devotion to God. There is no voluntary service. The love of our neighbors is not a measured, punch-the-clock proposition.

The God Movement is like a farmer who went out early in the morning to hire some field workers. Having settled on a wage of ten dollars a day, he sent them into the cotton field. Then about nine he went to town and saw others standing around idle. So he said to them, "Y'all go on out to the fields, and I'll pay you what's right." And they went. He did the same thing about noon, and again around three. Then about an hour before quitting time, he saw some others just hanging around. "Why have y'all been knocking around here all day doing nothing?" he asked. "Because nobody has hired us," they answered. "Okay, then y'all can go out to the cotton fields too," he said. At the end of the day the farmer said to his field boss, "Call the workers and pay them off, starting with those who came last and continuing to the first ones." Well, those who came an hour before quitting time were called up and were each paid ten dollars. Now those who got there first thing in the morning supposed that they would get much more, but when they were paid off, they too got ten dollars. At that, they raised a squawk against the farmer. "These latecomers didn't put in but one hour, and you've done the same by them as you did by us who stood in the hot sun and the scorching wind." But the farmer said to one of them, "Listen, buddy, I haven't mistreated you. Didn't you and I settle on ten dollars a day? Now pick up your pay and run along. I'm determined to give this last fellow exactly the same as you. Isn't it okay for me to do as I please with what's mine? Or are you bellyaching simply because I've been generous?" Matthew 20:1-15.

The Father meets the needs of His children with a grace that is sufficient. He does not expect us to bellyache when kingdom late-comers receive a salvation that is equal to our own. [3] And He does not expect us to balk at paying out to others, regardless of *their* deserts, the grace that we have received regardless of *our* deserts. To stand "in the hot sun and scorching wind" is, after all, a privilege for us, just as it was a privilege for the elder brother to slave all those years while the prodigal son was out squandering his inheritance. *Our obedience is not, in the ultimate sense, a reflection of our own effort; it is a reflection of God's graciousness to us.* If we don't see membership in God's family as a privilege, then the basic thrust of this writing has missed the mark. We are children of grace, or we are not God's children. We may proceed with the reshaping of our lives only to the extent that we can escape the jail of our own arrogance, which locks us into our old religion, wealth, and culture.

When I used to play "Monopoly," the board game which rewards sound business judgment and wise financial management, I always got a kick out of passing "Go" and collecting an automatic $200. Often it represented the only money I made during the entire game! And it was a gift that came to each player, regardless of skill, assuming that he or she could make a circuit of the board without landing in jail (or drawing that rare and terrible card that read: "Go directly to jail. *Do not* pass Go. *Do not* collect $200."). So this money was really a gift, even though it was provided for in the rules of the game and therefore anticipated.

The salary that the workers in the cotton field received at the end of the day was likewise a gift, because *just to be invited into the cotton field in the first place was a gift*. The complaint of the full-time workers, though it may have been justified in the narrow sense, was shortsighted and ill-advised. They forgot that they too had benefited from the employer's generosity when they were first given jobs.

Thus we see that the grace of God is meant to be comforting, but it may be discomforting as well. It demands that we receive it as grace, remember it as grace, and grant to others equal access. No one, of course, has an earned "right" to grace, and so we are all on the same slippery footing when it comes to our standing before God. When we resent God's generosity to others, we undermine and refuse the grace that comes to us. So we must judge others as we have been judged, we must forgive as we have been forgiven, and we must love as we have been loved. Thus we show ourselves to be the children of grace rather than the children of arrogance.

In Chapter Seven we discussed the parable of the zizania. We said that God could recognize imposter children even when it was hard for us to do so. But there is a way to recognize the child of arrogance within us even when it masquerades as the child of grace. Arrogance generates a proud thanksgiving: "O God, I thank You that I'm not like other people." Grace generates unabashed love. Arrogance is as "proper" and "dignified" as Simon, the church member described in connection with the parable of the two debtors. But the woman who was so uncivilized as to publicly bathe Jesus' feet with her tears proved by her *zealous* love the sincerity of her gratitude. [4]

A certain church member invited him home for dinner. He accepted and went into the church member's house and sat down. Then a shady lady of the town, who had heard that Jesus was being entertained at the church member's home, bought a bottle of high-priced perfume. She sat at his feet sobbing, and her tears began to wet his feet. She dried them with her long hair and kissed his feet and dabbed on some of the perfume.

When the church member who had invited him saw what was going on, he thought to himself, "If this fellow were a real man of God, he would recognize the kind of woman that's fondling him and know that she's a shady character."

Then Jesus said to him, "Simon, I want to talk with you about something."

He said, "Why sure, Doctor, go right ahead."

"Two men were in debt to a certain banker. One owed five hundred dollars, the other fifty.

When neither of them could pay up, the banker wrote off the debt of both. Which of the two would you think was the more grateful?"

Simon scratched his head and said, "Why, I suppose it was the one who was relieved of the larger debt."

Jesus said to him, "Right you are!" Then he turned to the lady and said to Simon, "Do you see this lady? When I came into your home, *you* didn't even give me *water* for my feet, but *she* has bathed my feet with her *tears* and dried them with her hair. You didn't even shake *hands* with me, but she, ever since she got here, has lovingly kissed my *feet*. So let me point out to you, Simon, that she has been relieved of a heavy load of sin, as evidenced by her great gratitude."

Then he said to her, "Your sins are gone."

And the guests at the table whispered among themselves, "Who does he think he is — forgiving sins!"

He said to the lady, "What you've just done has been the making of you; keep it up — with my blessing." Luke 7:36-50.

The grace of God is amazing because of the forgiveness that it offers to us: "Your sins are gone." It is amazing because of the discomfort it causes to those who witness its operation: "Who does he think he is — forgiving sins!" And it is amazing because it effectively binds us to a duty that otherwise would constitute overtime devotion: "What you've just done has been the making of you; *keep it up* — with my blessing."

9

COUNTING THE COST

Now we are working with a ray of hope. We
have come to grips with the subtle spirit of
arrogance within us. Jesus has knocked us off
our high horse, but He has done it to save
us, not to humiliate us. We have been stripped
of our illusions about our religion, our wealth,
and our culture, and we are at a critical junc-
ture in our journey toward the kingdom. We
must do more at this point than try to avoid
rattlesnakes.

When a filthy spirit comes out of a man, he
wanders through unwatered areas looking for a
home. Finding none, he says, "I'll go back to
my house that I left." He does so, and finds it
vacant, cleaned up, and painted. Then he goes
and rounds up seven other spirits more wicked
than himself, and they all move in and live
there. So the man is worse off at the end than
he was at the beginning. Matthew 12:43-45.

There is no virtue in an empty house; even
if it is cleaned up and painted. There is no virtue in a negative religion. So we must not be

content, even assuming that we have been able to avoid the pitfalls that the parables have pointed out to us. Jesus called the Pharisees "whitewashed tombs full of dead men's bones." Sometimes our view of proper religion amounts to little more than a removal of the bones. The parable of the empty house reinforces the idea that a creative passionate zeal is required if we are to gain the kingdom treasure. The purpose of this chapter is to probe and channel our enthusiasm in the right direction. Remember the seed that sprouted quickly only to wither in the shallow soil. Our zeal needs to be deep and persevering. We need to be aware of the extended cost involved in following Jesus. No degree of devotion can be too extreme a response to God's grace. Jesus pointed out the need for this kind of realistic reckoning during one of His journeys.

Quite a crowd was trailing him, and he turned and said to them, "If anyone is considering joining me, and does not break his attachment for father and mother and wife and children and brothers and sisters, indeed — for his own life — he simply cannot belong to my fellowship. Anyone who does not accept his own lynching and fall in behind me cannot belong to my fellowship.

"If any of you were intending to put up a building, wouldn't you first sit down and figure out the cost, so you could see if you had enough to finish it? Otherwise, you might lay out the foundation, and because you didn't have funds to go any further, people would begin making cracks about you, saying, 'This fellow is a great hand at starting things, but he can't carry through on them.'

"Or suppose a king were going out to battle against another king, wouldn't he first sit down and determine whether or not, with his ten thousand men, he could face an ememy of twenty thousand? If he figures he can't, then while there is still distance between them, he should send a delegation to seek for terms of peace.

"So that's the way it is with you. Everyone of you who doesn't throw in his entire fortune cannot belong to my fellowship." Luke 14:25- 33.

These parables of the incomplete building and the king's warfare point to the necessity for understanding the ultimate cost of discipleship. Jesus wants us to be fully aware of the implications of being children of God's grace. The context of these two parables outlines two of the requirements: "Anyone who does not accept his own lynching" and "who doesn't throw in his entire fortune cannot belong to my fellowship." Are we that serious about entering the kingdom that we sever ourselves from family ties, earthly security, and all of the dreams that we nurture for ourselves? Are we prepared to throw everything up in the air, including our schooling and our careers, our possessions and our ideas? Or are there certain relationships and realities that control us? God is giving us fair warning that He will touch us at every point to test whether our commitment is total. We can't bluff our way into His family. And we will be laughingstock to both God and ourselves if we permit anything to separate us from the consuming priority of the kingdom. Like the plight of the empty house, our fate then will be worse than if we had never taken Jesus seriously in the first place.

Jesus investigates our readiness by means of three short dramas recorded in Luke 9.

While they were going along the way, somebody said to him, "I'll live your life, regardless of where it takes me."

Jesus replied, "Foxes have dens, and the birds of the sky have nests, but the son of man has nowhere to hang his hat."

Then he said to another, "Share my life."

"Okay," he said, "but let me first discharge my family obligations."

Jesus told him, "Let the people of the world care for themselves, but *you*, you spend your time promoting the God Movement."

Still another said, "I will share your life, sir, but let me first work things out with my relatives."

To him Jesus replied, "No man who commits himself to a course of action, and then keeps looking for a way out of it, is fit material for the God Movement." Luke 9:57-62.

When Jesus said, "The son of man has nowhere to hang His hat," He was trying to show the totality of the demands of the kingdom. He was not going around looking for people that He could bait by offering a better job:

"You can follow Me."

"How much are You paying? I'm getting $100 a week."

"Well, I'll give you $125."

That isn't the way that the Lord gathered apostles or disciples. He made it clear to them that it was going to be costly, just as it had cost Him, and that you might not have any place that you could call home.

The person in the second drama, in response to Jesus' request to share life, literally said, "Let me first go and bury my daddy."

And Jesus said to him, "Let the dead bury their own dead, but you go and proclaim the new order of the Spirit."

At first sight it might appear that Jesus was being rather rude to this fellow. Here he's saying, "My father died. Can I go to the funeral? I'll come right after the funeral. I'll be right with You." But we misunderstand if we think that's what he means, because this man's father wasn't dead. He was still very much alive, and kicking around. What did they want to bury him for, if he was still alive? Well, in those days, the expression "to bury somebody" meant to live with them until they died, and then put them away, and then you were free. It might take you ten years to bury somebody. To bury your father meant to discharge your earthly obligations to your father.

In the first situation, Jesus places the obligation to the kingdom above your material welfare. In the second one, He places it above your relationship to society. Even your father and your relatives can't take priority over the demands of the kingdom of God. If your father can't take precedence, how much less could your friends? So, the kingdom is not a matter of what other important people are going to say or think. Your loyalty goes to God.

You can't come face-to-face with the kingdom of God and respond, "I like this idea of the God Movement, but, you know, I got a spouse and some children. I gotta raise them, and let me get them up out of the way and off to college and get them through college and let me get my house paid for and all these things. And then, when I get free from all these obligations, I think it'd be nice to retire into the kingdom of God." Jesus said, "The kingdom of God just isn't an old folks home. You don't retire into it. I want you to get busy NOW."

A third would-be disciple said, "Lord, I will follow You, but first let me go home and draw up a contract with my kinfolks, or with my brothers and sisters." Some translations simply record that he wanted to say, "Farewell," but the Greek carries a much more extensive idea than that. This fellow is really saying, "I want to join this movement, but I don't like this idea of having to give up all I've got. Now, my pappy is quite well off and he's gonna leave a nice estate when he dies and I wanna go back there and get a lawyer to draw me up an agreement that if I go off with You, I am still in the family inheritance, and I get my share. I don't wanna take the risk of this God Movement. I wanna protect myself."

In other words, he wanted an escape hatch so that if it folded up, he'd have something to go back on. He wanted what we call a "scat-hole." Down south we cut a little square hole in the bottom of the door so the cat can have some way to come and go; and when you say, "Scat," he's got some way to go without you gittin' up and openin' the door for him. This boy wanted him a scat-hole so that if the sailin' got rough, and he had to get out of the situation real quick, he could scat.

A lot of folks don't wanna cut loose of everything and jump into this thing. They wanna say, "Well, what if this thing folds up?"

We had a lady one time come and visit us at Koinonia. She was a very lonely lady. I'd say she was in her early forties. She came up in her old jalopy car and she was rather shabbily dressed and we talked to her for several days. She said, "You know, I like it here. I believe I'd like to just live here."

We said, "That's fine, we'd be glad to have ya."

And she said, "What do I do to join up?"

"Well, just come on and join with us. I presume you don't have much. You can just stay on."

She said, "Oh, well, I have a good bit of property down in New Orleans."

"How much do you have'?"

"Oh, I guess I own maybe $90,000 worth."

"Well, the first thing you'll have to do is get rid of that."

She said, "What do you mean? I can't do that!"

"But then you can't come here."

"But I can't give away my possessions. Suppose this thing were to fold up and I had given away everything I owned. Then where would I be?"

I said, "Then you'd be in the same place as the rest of us would be."

"But, can't I bring my money and put it in here?"

"No, ma'am, this is the one place you can't put it."

"Why? Don't you all need it?"

"Yes, ma'am, we sure do."

"How come I can't put it in here?"

"Well," I said, "one reason is you got more money than all the rest of us put together, and if you want to put all your money in here, the first thing we'd do would be to sit down under a pecan tree and start discussing theology. We need to work. We don't need that kinda money. It'll make us lazy and it'll make theologians out of us, and we don't want that to happen to us. And," I said, "in the next place, you'll be, in your mind, sort of our guardian angel, and you'll expect each of us to tip our hats to you and thank you for what marvelous things you've done for us. We don't tip our hats to anybody, and we don't want you comin' in here with a lot of money. And, in the last place, the reason you can't bring it here's because you look like a very lonely person, and unless I miss my guess, the only friends you've ever had have been those who have wanted to help you spend your money."

She said, "You're right. I don't believe I've ever had a real friend who loved me for what

115

I am. They've always loved my money."

"And if you bring that money here, you'll always have a sneaking suspicion that the reason we wanted you here was not for what you are, but because of your money. And the only way you can get a clear answer to that is to go sell your possessions and give the money to the poor, and come back here without a dime, and then you'll know whether we love you for what you are or for what you have. You'll get your answer."

She said, "I, I just can't do it," and she got in her old jalopy and drove off.

As she did, I turned to my wife and we almost said in unison, "There goes the female rich young ruler." She wanted a scat-hole. She wanted an escape. She wanted to trust her little $90,000 when she needed to learn to trust in God, whose riches are untold.

There is a sense in which this total giving is a prerequisite for entering the kingdom of God. When we enter the kingdom we sign over to God all of our possessions and all of our energies. But there is also a sense in which our emptying of ourselves is a gradual unfolding of our lives within the kingdom. Jesus gave up His life when He decided to become Immanuel, God with us. He carried out that commitment during a thirty-three-year ordeal that culminated at the cross. The question of when He actually died — whether in Bethlehem, at His baptism, at Golgotha, or gradually throughout His ministry — is academic. [1] The point is that

116

His death was inevitable. The implications of total commitment are set in motion. We enter the arena knowing that we will never emerge alive and intact. This entrance, this "death," is the beginning of discipleship. We have begun to respond to our overdose of grace. The ray of hope has become, for us, a rainbow.

10

TRADE WITH THESE IDEAS

The hope for liberation becomes a reality for us when we *act* upon the ideas that the parables have imparted to us.

A man had two boys. He went to the older one and said, "My boy, go work in the orchard today." He said, "Will do, Pop," but he never did. Then he went to the younger one and told him the same thing. But the boy said, "I won't go." Afterwards he felt like a heel, and did go. Which of the two obeyed his father? Matthew 21:28-31.

Attitude and motivation are an important part of discipleship, but action is emphasized in this brief story. Jesus was aware of the temptation to "spiritualize" obedience. We feel compassionate, we desire justice. But such emotions are not in themselves sufficient. George MacDonald has said, "Talking and not doing is dry rot." Sincere grappling with ideas is not the same as obedience. Praying for God's blessing on others is not the same as giving it or being it to others. If we act without correctly verbalizing our intentions we are closer to the kingdom than if we fail to act despite our noble proclamations and inclinations of the heart. We have to do more than mouth the ideas of the God Movement. We have to trade with these ideas.

It's like a businessman who was leaving town for a long time and called in his assistants and turned over his investments to them. He made one responsible for about five hundred thousand dollars, another two hundred thousand, and another a hundred thousand — according to each one's ability — and then he left town. Right away the man with the five hundred grand got to work and made five hundred more. The man with the two hundred grand did the same and made another two hundred. But the guy with the hundred G's went and rented a safe-deposit box and put his boss' money in it. After a long time the boss returned and called his assistants together for an accounting. The one with the five hundred thousand brought his other five hundred thousand and said, "Sir, you let me have five hundred grand; look, I've made another five hundred." The boss said, "Splendid, you good and responsible worker! You were diligent with the smaller sum; I'll entrust you with a larger one. You'll be a partner in my business." Then the one with the two hundred G's came and said, "Sir, you let me have two hundred thousand; look, I've made another two hundred." The boss said, "Splendid, you good and responsible worker! You were diligent with the smaller sum, I'll entrust you with a larger one. You'll be a partner in my business." Well, the hundred-grand man came up and said, "Sir, I know you are a hard-nosed man, squeezing pennies you haven't yet made and expecting a profit before the ink has dried. I was plain scared to take any chances, so I rented a safe-deposit box and put your money in it. Look, you've got every cent." But his boss replied, "You sorry, ornery bum! You knew that I squeeze pennies I haven't yet made, and expect profits before the ink dries. Then you should have turned my money over to the bank so that upon my return I would get back at least my principal with interest. So then, y'all take the money away from him and give it to the one with the million. For it will be given to everyone who has the stuff, and he'll have plenty, but the man who doesn't have the stuff will have even what he has taken away from him. Now as for this useless critter, throw him in the back alley. That'll give him something to moan and groan about." Matthew 25:14-30.

Jesus tells this story to His followers while they are on their way to Jerusalem, near the end of His ministry. It was the last week, and Jesus had been talking about the revolution and so forth, and His disciples were all excited. And they were wondering whether they were going to have a press conference, to take over the airport, and the telephone exchange, and there was excitement in the air. Perhaps the revolution was about to burst out immediately with overwhelming force. And to answer that kind of thinking, Jesus told the parable of the talents.

I've heard so many sermons preached on this idea, "Give your talents to the Lord." They got that thing backwards. The Lord gives His talents

to us. A talent is not some skill. We go around
saying, "He's a great athlete. He should con-
secrate his talent to the Lord. She's a great organist. She should be an organist for the Lord."
But this isn't what Jesus is saying.

What are these talents? Are they money? No,
Jesus had no money to give. What did He have?
What is the stock-in-trade of a great teacher? It's
his ideas, his concepts, his teachings. He leaves
them to His followers. All these three years He
has been "talenting" them. Now He's saying,
"You want me to come in here and pull some
angels out of the sky and set up a revolution?
Oh, no. I've been giving you over all these
months together the currency of the kingdom,
and if it comes, it's gonna come by your doin'
business with what I've turned over to you."

To us He says, "I've turned over to you the
idea of brotherhood."

And some of us can say, "Yes, Lord, I got out
and dealt with that idea and multiplied it."

But others of us turn in an accounting like this:
"Yes, Lord, I remember you talkin' about brotherhood but, You know, I was scared. I started
to preach a sermon on that on race relations
Sunday, but Deacon Jones said, 'Hmmm.' You
know I didn't want to upset the deacon. No
point breakin' up your church. Besides, Deacon
Jones, he's one of our major tithers, and he's
got something to tithe. So, Lord, I was scared,
I was scared of this whole proposition and I
buried this idea of brotherhood."

"I gave to you the idea of peace."

"Yes, Lord. But You don't understand the

*civilization we live in. You gotta talk force.
Force is the only language most folks understand today. Really, it's the only language people
know how to talk. So, Lord, I had a chance to
witness for peace, but I was kind of scared somebody might identify me with these flower children, and I just buried the whole thought."*

We've all been given ideas, perhaps not in
equal proportion to others. Maybe we haven't
done any postgraduate work, but we've got hold
of some explosive ideas. But we say, "I might
lose out tradin' on these. I might lose my neck
or my job or my house."

And we're right. This is risk capital Jesus has
given to us. But that doesn't excuse us from
activity. This little ol' fellow in the parable didn't
steal anything from his boss. In fact, he restored
everything. He just didn't do what he was told.
Discussing talents isn't a test of talent activity.
This assistant had read a book on talent preservation; he had read a book on economics; he was
quite knowledgeable on the present value of a
talent; he held conferences on inflation and de-
flation of the talent. He just never got to work.
He never put it out there and traded with it.

Now let me tell you, we don't have much more
time to do business with the kingdom ideas. It's
later than we think. We've caught a glimpse of
the gold in God's storehouse. The time of harvest is here. If we don't get off our back ends
and start doin' somethin' with these ideas, God
Almighty is gonna take these talents that He's
turned over to the church and give them to a
people that will bring forth the fruits. And they

might not be a people that we will agree with.

This punch parable is one of Jesus' ways of saying, "You better get up and git! I've given you these ideas, turned over to you My treasure. Now, what are you gonna do with them? You gonna wrap them up in some theological junk or are you gonna get out in the streets and do business with these ideas?"

What are these ideas that are so crucial? Our examination of the parables gives us at least the following new directions for our lives:

(1) *The kingdom of God is now.* The parables communicate the urgency of the moment. They focus our attention upon this life — the grace we receive and the obedience we render.

(2) *The Kingdom of God is a gradual process.* We will be consistently disheartened until we are able to accept this reality.

(3) *The process involves suffering and powerlessness.* Our continuing goal is to know Christ by sharing His humble beginnings and experiencing His servanthood.

(4) *The process is the result of our dependency upon God.* He is our Father. We are His children. Our lives are a response to and a reflection of His grace.

These ideas transform our lives as we permit them to condition our outlook on life and as we act upon them. We can grasp their future implications by considering the twin parables of the mustard seed and the leaven.

Then he said, "What is the God Movement

like, and with what shall I compare it? It's
like a mustard seed which a man plants in his
garden, and it keeps growing until it becomes
a big bush, and the birds in the sky make its
branches their home."

And again he said, "With what shall I compare the God Movement? It's like yeast which
a housewife mixes in three cups of flour until
it all rises." Luke 13:18-21.

*The mustard seed is the smallest of seeds,
and when it grows it becomes a bush, big
enough for birds to come and build their nests
in it. The old birds probably flew over that
seed many a time and didn't even think it was
worth noticing; it just wasn't even worth peck-
ing at. They passed it by. And yet it began to
sprout. The seed is that which has life resi-
dent in it. And there's a big difference between
a seed and a grain of sand. You plant a grain
of sand and it doesn't matter how much rain-
fall and sunshine you have, you're not going
to get an increase. But you plant a seed and
you'll get some action. Jesus is saying that
these kingdom ideas are viable ideas; they're
not sterile. Now, if we could just get hold of
some of these ideas in some of our pulpits,
it could blow these pulpits and church buildings
all to pieces.*

*The seed is a viable kind of thing that has
a habit of pushing its way even against great
difficulties. Just a few weeks back we got
through planting peanuts. You put the peanut seed two or three inches under the ground.
We had a big, hard, packing rain. I thought,*

*"Oh my goodness, that little old peanut seed
will never to able to break that hard crust."
But a few days later we went out there and
there was a tiny Spanish peanut seed lifting
a clod of dirt twenty times bigger than it was,
just pushin', sayin,' "Get out of the way, clod,
I'm movin' to God." And that little old seed
came on out of there. You can't keep life
down. So Jesus says that if you have kingdom
life in you, you move on in spite of the most
terrible difficulties and hindrances. On and on
the kingdom goes, beginning* now. *The
power, he says, is like leaven that just reaches
out and goes through the whole lump.*

This fact that the kingdom of God is a gradual process does not mean that it is not an
urgent process. The idea of urgency has been
implanted within us by several parables that
have already been discussed, especially the parables of the hidden treasure and the pearl of
great price, along with the parable of the man
on his way to court. But we should not em-
bark upon our lives of discipleship thinking
that our implementation of mercy and justice will reach immediate fruition. We plant
powerful seeds of love. They work silently
and persistently to accomplish God's will. There
is no fanfare, no world-beating display of
strength. But within the humblest act of obedience to God there is the assurance of victory.

The irony of the parable of the mustard seed
is that the birds that might have initially
ravaged the man's garden remain to enjoy

its benefits — they nest in the branches of its vegetation. Even our enemies will be won over to the kingdom. Not only does the small produce the great, but a narrow hostility is swallowed up by a more comprehensive fellowship. When you see that even those who "call you names, and harass you and tell all kinds of false tales on you" are your eventual brothers and sisters, then you will not seek revenge, but will be "cheerful and good-humored." [2] When you ask, even though you are only one person with impure motivation; and when you seek, even though you are acting on behalf of only one of the world's needy; and when you knock, even though you are pounding on the door of only one of the world's many oppressors, you are nonetheless initiating a process that will result in justice rolling on like a river and righteousness like an ever-flowing stream. [3] As it was in the parable of the sower, so it will be in your life: one solitary sustained response to the grace of God will bring forth a hundred, or sixty, or thirty times the initial investment.

So we must trade with the idea that our actions are invincible, even though they may be surrounded by a sea of inhumanity and godlessness for as long as we live. And we must trade with the idea that our own lives represent the initial lump that is leavened. Transformation is possible. We can be "raised" now to the new reality of life within the kingdom as we give ourselves to God, and as He gives us the power to become His children.

126

The ultimate victory of our course sustains us, but we should not be concerned with the *strategy* of victory.

This is what the kingdom of God is like. A man throws seed on the land. Night and day, while he sleeps, when he is awake, the seed is sprouting and growing; *how, he does not know.* Of its own accord the land produces first the shoot, then the ear, then the full grain in the ear. Mark 4:26-28, *Jerusalem Bible* (emphasis added).

We loose the seeds of mercy upon the world. They do their work. We are the bearers and sowers of the kingdom of God, not the architects. God has scattered us in the same way that we are to scatter His truth.

But we also *are* the seed of the kingdom. The leaven that is placed within the meal is the leaven of our own witness. We are the salt of the earth and the light of the world. [4] And the most devastating idea that God asks us to incarnate is captured in this instruction:

Jesus then said to his students, "If a man wants to walk my way, he must abandon self, accept his lynching, and share my life. For the person who aims to save his life will lose it, and the one who loses his life for my cause will find it. Matthew 16:24-25.

So we do not merely *observe* the gradual process of the kingdom coming, we also *participate* by losing our lives. The impact of this concept leaves our old way of thinking in a shambles. How could there be a sharper contrast between our past life and our present life? How could there be a higher cost? How could there be a greater love?

> I tell you, most solemnly,
> unless a wheat grain falls on the ground and dies,
> it remains only a single grain;
> but if it dies,
> it yields a rich harvest.
> Anyone who loves his life loses it;
> anyone who hates his life in this world
> will keep it for the eternal life. John 12:24-25,
> *Jerusalem Bible.*

This is why we can never incorporate and organize and strategize the God Movement. We would be too inclined by our own natures to promote and perpetuate our own existence. We would not allow ourselves to give our organization, our possessions, and our lives away.

Everything has to be lovely. Everything has to work. Everything has to be practical. Everything has to come out right. The story has to end, ". . . and they lived happily ever after." And we don't want a story that doesn't end that way. So anything that comes in to break up the happy ending — to end the pragmatic way we live — why, we just don't want it. We want to get rid of a God who calls people to die for Him, whose own life winds up on a cross. He just isn't the kind of God we want around.

But Jesus said that the life of His disciples would be life in the shadow of a cross. It's a dying kind of living. He said that you don't know whether it will work or not. Why don't you break off a few chunks of life and try? You experiment with everything else. Break off a few years — a chunk — of your life, and give it in this bold experiment and see what happens.

If we are only concerned to provide for our supposed personal righteousness and to maintain the cleanliness and composure of our empty house, then we will not venture out with these ideas. We will be content to bury them beneath our preaching or to adopt them as the playthings of our minds. To trade with the idea of dying we must welcome the persecution and poverty that come our way as a result of our unconditional servanthood.

Servanthood is the kingdom process whose small beginnings carry us through suffering to resurrection. All we really want is "to know Christ and the power of his resurrection and to share his sufferings by reproducing the pattern of his death." [5] We bring good news to the poor, and we help the oppressed, but in these works of mercy we become the poor and the oppressed. This is our dying, and the finding of our lives.

THE WORKS OF MERCY

In the chapter on "Disturbing the Peace" we considered the close relationship between justice and mercy. God has been merciful to us, and we must reflect that mercy in our relations with others as a matter of fairness. In that chapter we focused upon the pursuit of justice. In this chapter we shall focus upon the works of mercy. But it is well to keep in mind that the difference in terminology and content is somewhat arbitrary. One can't love tenderly without acting justly. And if the works of mercy are carried out, they will be sufficient in themselves to disturb the peace even though yelling and pounding and persistent nagging may not immediately enter into the picture.

Jesus found Himself in trouble because He took the idea of mercy seriously. He traded with the idea that the necessity for compassion overrode the protocol considerations that were of paramount importance to the religious establishment. "Is it proper to eat with sinners?" "Is it proper to heal on the sabbath?" For Jesus, mercy always took precedence over any human concept of propriety.

This chapter is entitled "The *Works* of Mercy" because that's what mercy is in the New Testament. It is not an inward feeling of pity or compassion; it is a roll-up-your-sleeves endeavor. We have come a long way together through the parables. We have left behind our old lives and we have embraced new ideas. Now we are off the drawing board and out of the classroom. We have counted the cost and have given our lives. At some point during the long night of our prayer and struggle we have crossed an invisible boundary. We have put our hands to the plow and we shall never look back. We are God's new farming partners, and we are scattering seeds of mercy that will eventually grow and nourish all of our friends and enemies alike.

Mercy is not an abstract consideration in the teaching of Jesus. *We must be careful, therefore, not to substitute analysis for implementation.* Mercy is not the subject for our doctoral dissertation, it is the outpouring of our sweat and tears. We must not fall into the trap of the adult Bible class teacher who was more concerned with theory than with practice:

One day a teacher of an adult Bible class got up and tested him with this question: "Doctor, what does one do to be saved?"

Jesus replied, "What does the Bible say? How do you interpret it?"

The teacher answered, "Love the Lord your God with all your heart and with all your soul and with all your physical strength and with all your mind; and love your neighbor as yourself."

"That is correct," answered Jesus. "Make a habit of this and you'll be saved."

But the Sunday school teacher, trying to save face, asked, "But . . . er . . . but . . . just who *is* my neighbor?"

Then Jesus laid into him and said, "A man was going from Atlanta to Albany and some gangsters held him up. When they had robbed him of his wallet and brand-new suit, they beat him up and drove off in his car, leaving him unconscious on the shoulder of the highway.

"Now it just so happened that a white preacher was going down that same highway. When he saw the fellow, he stepped on the gas and went scooting by.

"Shortly afterwards a white Gospel song leader came down the road, and when he saw what had happened, he too stepped on the gas.

"Then a black man traveling that way came upon the fellow, and what he saw moved him to tears. He stopped and bound up his wounds as best he could, drew some water from his water-jug to wipe away the blood and then laid him on the back seat. He drove on into Albany and took him to the hospital and said to the nurse, 'You all take good care of this white man I found on the highway. Here's the only two dollars I got, but you all keep account of what he owes, and if he can't pay it, I'll settle up with you when I make a pay-day.'

"Now if you had been the man held up by the gangsters, which of these three — the white preacher, the white song leader, or the black man — would you consider to have been your neighbor?"

The teacher of the adult Bible class said, "Why of course, the nig — I mean, er . . . well, er . . . the one who treated me kindly."

Jesus said, "Well, then, *you* get going and start living like that!" Luke 10:25-37.

Jesus was dealing at a time when racial prejudice was terrific. Jews and Samaritans had no dealings with each other, and He had to be very careful with what He said. One day, a fellow stopped Him. "By the way, Master, I want to ask you a question. What's the first and great commandment?" This fellow was a scribe, and a scribe was a combination of Bible teacher and an expert in religious law. So we might call him a lawyer in addition to being a Sunday school teacher.

This young lawyer just got out of law school and he had that question on his final exams, and he wanted to see if Jesus knew it. And Jesus said, "Well, Colonel, how do you read it?" He kinda threw it back at him. And this lawyer started spoutin' it off. He'd learned it in class.

Jesus responded to his recitation by saying, "You've got it right, Colonel. You've got it right. You live that way and you will have life."

"Oh," the lawyer said, "Now, I didn't mean I was gonna live by it. I just love to quote it." You know how some people quote Scripture. They don't mean any harm by it; they love to hear it. They just don't want to live

133

by it. And the lawyer began to pick a little flaw. You know, lawyers can get you by hittin' on technical details. So this lawyer said, "Well, there's one little point there that needs clarifying. Who is my neighbor?" That young lawyer should have known that the preachers had all agreed that anybody was your neighbor provided he was one of the pure blue-blooded aristocratic faithful. As long as he was white, Anglo-Saxon, and Protestant, he was your neighbor. If anybody wasn't, you could give him the works. You didn't have to love him. Now, Jesus said you had to love your neighbor, and this lawyer thought he would create a name for himself by putting Jesus on the spot. Jesus had gone around doin' a lot of preachin' to the Samaritans, and this lawyer thought, "If that guy preaches that social equality stuff right here in Jerusalem, there's gonna be enough of these red necks to really tar and feather Him. We'll fix Him up."

So Jesus said, "Well, Colonel, I'll tell you a little story." And here Jesus is hiding His truth. The lawyer knows he's gonna catch it, but he doesn't know how or when. He's on, and he's gotta ride, and Jesus is pickin' up speed and he can't jump off.

In the course of the story Jesus talked first about a priest. But down south we don't have many priests. Everybody down there is either a Methodist or a Baptist unless somebody's been tinkering with him. So we'll call him a preacher. As he whizzed by the beaten man by the side of the road, his homiletic mind probably

134

made the following outline: (1) I do not know
the man. (2) I do not wish to get involved in
any court proceedings. (3) I don't want to get
blood on my new upholstering. (4) The man's
lack of proper clothing would embarrass me
upon my arrival in town. (5) And finally, bre-
thren, a minister must never be late for a revival meeting. (And he was going to preach that
evening on "God Is Love.")

Next, Jesus mentioned the Levite. What is a
Levite? Those folks standin' out there in front
of Jesus knew what a Levite was. In those days
there was the Levitical tribe, and all of the
descendants of Levi were the preachers. You
didn't get a call to preach then. You were born
a preacher by bein' in the Levitical tribe. But
Levi had so many descendants down through
the centuries that pretty soon there were more
preachers than there were pulpits. They had to
find other work for these Levites to do, and they
became assistant ministers. Then, when they
filled up all those slots, they became ministers
of music. Now, this fellow perhaps was the minister of music, or maybe we'd call him the hymn
leader. He was going to help in the revival
songfest. He saw the injured man, but he had
told the junior choir to meet him half an hour
early. He wanted to teach 'em a little junior
song: "Brighten the corner where you are."
Besides, you can start a meetin' without a
preacher, but you got to have somebody there
to lead the singing.

If the preacher and the minister of music
aren't going to stop, who is going to help this

poor fellow? Jesus said that another traveler came along. He was driving an old Model T. They say those were the most religious automobiles ever made. They shook the devil out of more folks than any other car. I can see it now: great big front end, each time the back tire went around it would go "ahump, ahump," window shades flapping in the wind, and old magnesium lights. He came churning along at about fifteen to twenty miles per hour, and he stopped. Of course, he didn't have much trouble stopping, but he stopped. "Who could it be?" the lawyer asked. "Who was it?"

And Jesus said he was a black man. [1] He got out of his car and saw this man lying there. And he might have said something along this line: "Sombody's robbed you. Yeah, I know about that; I've been robbed too. And they beat you up bad; I know, I've been beat up too. And everybody just went right on by and left you here hurting; yeah, I know, they pass me by too."

He drove him into town, passed the revival meeting where they were singing, "Love lifted me," and took him into the hospital. He paid as much as he could toward the man's bill, then he promised to pay whatever was necessary upon his return.

Jesus turned to the lawyer and said to him, "Would you tell me, please, who was the neighbor?"

And this lawyer, unwilling even to say the word, drew his robes of righteousness about him and said, "Well, I, I suppose, I suppose it was

136

that guy who showed mercy."

Jesus said, "You got it right. Now you go and
start living that way *yourself."*

Now *we* have to get going and start living
that way. To be merciful means to do whatever
the situation demands, to pay whatever the man
owes. We like to figure out in advance what
we have to give up. What is mercy going to
cost us? But true mercy doesn't ask for limits,
it only asks for opportunity. There are no outer
limits to discipleship. We have already crossed
the bridge of total dispossession when we entered the kingdom. It only remains for us now
to flesh out our servanthood. It is too late to
ask questions about whether we really want to
die or not.

If you want to know if mercy is actually the
currency of the kingdom, then you must do it. [2]
Mercy is spontaneous, not planned. There
is not time for calculating possible risk or
effect. What does it matter if, in the process
of helping the victim beside the road, you yourself become a victim? If you are robbed and
slain, then you only receive the greater opportunity to be a child of your Father, who was
also robbed and slain when He stopped by you
in your distress. Mercy is not traditional, not
token, not sterile. *Mercy is the creative risk
of unlimited involvement.* Mercy seldom gets
off the ground when we approach it from the
standpoint of a hypothetical question. It begins when we see our world as a world of
neighbors. And it culminates when we act

toward the person in need as if that person were actually Christ Himself. This is the thrust of the parable of the last judgment.

When the son of man starts his revolution with all his band around him, then he will assume authority. And all the nations will be assembled before him, and he will sort them out, like a farmer separating his cows from his hogs, penning the cows on the right and the hogs on the left. Then the Leader of the Movement will say to those on his right, "Come, you pride of my Father, share in the Movement that was set up for you since creation; for I was hungry and you shared your food with me; I was thirsty and you shared your water with me; I was a stranger and you welcomed me, ragged and you clothed me, sick and you nursed me; I was in jail, and you stood by me." Then the people of justice will answer, "Sir, when did we see you hungry and share our food, or thirsty and share our water? When did we see you a stranger and welcome you, or ragged and clothe you? When did we see you sick or in jail, and stand by you?" And the Leader of the Movement will reply, "When you did it to one of these humblest brothers of mine, you did it to me."

Then he will say to those on his left, "Get away from me, you fallen skunks, and into the flaming hell reserved for the Confuser and his crowd. For I was hungry and you shared nothing with me; I was thirsty and you gave me no water; I was a stranger and you didn't welcome me, ragged and you didn't clothe me, sick and in jail, and you didn't stand by me." Then these too will ask, "Sir, when did we see you hungry or thirsty or a stranger or ragged or sick or in jail, and do nothing about your needs?" Then he'll answer, "When you failed one of these humblest people you failed me." These will take an awful beating, while the just ones will have the joy of living. Matthew 25:31-46.

When Jesus said to those on His right, "Come, you pride of My Father, share in the Movement that was set up for you since creation," He was saying, "This revolution is not a fad. The kingdom has its roots in eternity and it has been growing and sprouting for a long time. You all come in and enter into it."

I think Jesus was talkin' about now. The kingdom is a contemporary life, not a future life, of compassion, of sharing, of serving, of identification, of empathy. He said, "I was hungry and you fed Me," and they said, "When did we see You?" They didn't say, "Yes, Lord, I got that here somewhere. I sent that in with the last annual report. Let's see, oh, yeah, 219 gallons of water, 300 gallons of milk. That's pretty good, isn't it Lord? Right nice."

"I was sick and you came unto Me."

"Yeah, I had to make a few phone calls and I got that here: 3,019 phone calls; that's pretty good."

You know, we'd have it all codified, ready to send in. But these people on the right-hand side had made it such a habit that they *were no longer able to keep records. Paul, in his great song of love in 1 Corinthians 13 — I forget how it is in the ordinary English — but in the cotton-pickin' kind he said, "Love keeps no books." And I think this is what Jesus was talking about. These people have risen above being statistical Christians. If you're still in the bookkeeping business, you better reexamine your love. You're a child; you're dealing with childish things.*

He said to these people, "I expect from My followers a kind of life that identifies them. I was thirsty and you knew how to respond." Now this is the kind of thing the Christians, many times, seem to be so dumb about. When they see a man who's thirsty, they haven't got sense enough to give him water. They bring him a hymnal. Or, to take an even more ridiculous example, a Baptist church I know installed a $25,000 fountain on its front lawn. That thing has the capacity of a thousand gallons a minute. That's enough water for any Baptist. A thousand gallons a minute! We Baptists don't do things half way. And the people come and Jesus says, "I was thirsty." "Yeah, Lord, and we built you a circulatin' fountain." Now, imagine spendin' $25,000 of God Almighty's good money to put up a circulatin' fountain when some people don't even have runnin' water in their kitchens! Can you imagine people being that idiotic?

Jesus expects Christians to know how to respond. "I was thirsty and you gave Me water. I was hungry and you gave Me a dissertation

on the fifth horse in the Book of Revelation."
*It seems to me that Christians gotta know that
a hungry man gotta have bread, a thirsty man
gotta have water, and a sick man gotta have
a doctor, and a man in jail gotta have somebody
to come to him.*

*I was preachin' down in Florida in February,
in a rather big town down there, and I was in-
formed that a big church had just spent $40,-
000 to plant a "Flowers-of-the-Bible" garden.
They went through the Bible and they found
where it says "roses of Sharon." So they go to
Sharon, wherever that is, and they get 'em some
roses. And then they read where it says "the
lilies of the valley." And they go where the
valley is and get 'em some lilies. And those
people spent $40,000 on exotic plants from all
over the world to make a "Flowers-of-the-
Bible" garden so that people could walk
through that garden and smell the roses of
Sharon and look at the lilies of the valley. I
think somebody ought to put some cages up
so they can have the birds of the air, especially if they'd stand under one and look up. I
think that would be the most devotional experience they could have.*

*In that same city, I visited a day-care center
with approximately seventy-five little flowers
in it. They were black flowers. Their play-
ground, I give you my word, was hardly as
big as a garage. They had no equipment. And
here those idiotic "Christians" spent $40,000
on exotic flowers and not one dime for God's
little flowers. Can you imagine it?*

*So I said to the people that I was preachin'
to, "You all have been complainin' to me all
week about how ineffective the church is and
how dead religion is. I want to make you a
proposition. As soon as this thing is over, all
of you get your grubbin' tools and we'll go up
there and grub up that "Flowers-of-the-Bible"
garden, and I think we'll have a little excitement goin' on as a protest of people being
so blind as to spend God Almighty's money in
that way."*

*And I couldn't find a soul who was in-
terested in grubbing. And I didn't grub either.
I've been ashamed of it ever since.*

We have seen that mercy is not a program
that we devise while we're praying or medita-
ting or reading the Bible. It is an action that
we take while we're walking the road. Mercy
is *now*, not a future point or a five-year plan.

In the last part of this excerpt from Clarence
we can see that the demand for justice is likewise occasioned by experience rather than by
analysis. We need to keep our eyes open, to listen for the sounds of human anguish, to go
slow enough to stop wherever a work of mercy
waits for us so that we can take the opportunity to carry out the compassion of God. If we
follow that work of mercy to conclusion, we will
often be led into the yelling and pounding and
nagging dimension of justice. The serious
implementation of mercy creates a strong soli-
darity among ourselves, Jesus, and the oppressed. We see ourselves and, more signifi-

142

cantly, we see our Lord, among the seventy-five "little flowers" at the day-care center. We hunger and thirst for justice to the extent that we become the victims of injustice. Clarence "couldn't find a soul who was interested in grubbing" because he couldn't find a soul who was seriously interested in mercy.

What would have happened if the good Samaritan, the black man in the Cotton Patch version, had taken his unconscious friend to the hospital and found the attendant asleep and the doors locked? He would have done what justice required, even as he had already begun to do what mercy required.

The world has always respected and honored "good" people, because "good" people always work for change from within the system. By their participation they unconsciously endorse the acceptability of the world order and legitimize its processes. The world order sees these "good" people as friends. But the kingdom of God stands as a witness against the world order. And the mercy and justice of God spell the end of this world's way of doing things. Our culture has been able to immunize itself against the church by forging an unholy alliance with it. But the powers of this world can never appease the foolishness of the family of God. The children of the Father trade with the idea that to lose one's life in the works of mercy and justice is to gain one's life. It is a dangerous idea, and it makes us dangerous people: Christians on the loose!

So the parables have had to lead us, kicking and screaming perhaps, out of an old way of life into a new set of values and relationships. We have very little in common with "good" people, mercy has very little in common with humanitarianism, and justice has very little in common with reform. We must go beyond goodness to the actual laying down of our lives. We do not want a reshuffling of the cards. We want to start playing with a totally new deck — living/dying a totally new life — because the old cards are marked against the purposes of God no matter how they're shuffled.

THE PARABOLIC LIFE

To seek the kingdom is to seek justice, and
to love God is to love our neighbor. To seek
justice is to be merciful (where seeds of mercy
may be planted) and to resist injustice (where
illegitimate structures of oppression prevent
the exercise of mercy). To love our neighbor
is to become our neighbor's servant. Here we
have the interlocking pieces of discipleship:
justice and mercy; servanthood and resistance.

The grace of the Father reshapes our lives.
Our attitude toward God becomes thanksgiving.
Our understanding of ourselves becomes
humility. Our response to our brothers and
sisters is from the posture of servanthood,
wherein we incarnate and convey to them
God's mercy. And our approach to the ideology
of oppression is resistance, wherein we raise a
witness against the culture of militarism, greed,
and prejudice.

How do we raise this witness? The final concern of this book is to help us put the teachings
of the parables into the context of a parabolic
life. Jesus not only taught in parables, He lived

a parable. To witness for mercy and justice is more than a matter of words, of course, but it is also more than a matter of individual good deeds. It is a matter of life situation.

Jesus spoke about loving one another, sometimes in parables and sometimes in straight teaching. Jesus also performed many acts of love. But what was Jesus' life all about at its deepest level? Did His ministry consist of the stories He told, the lives He changed, the sins He forgave, the diseases He healed, and the tables He overturned? No. When we see Jesus' ministry as only a series of teachings and accomplishments, we see how it was frustrated — by the nine lepers who didn't return to give thanks; [1] by the money-changers who renewed their Temple trade after Jesus had thrown them out; [2] by Lazarus, who was raised from the dead only to die again; [3] and by the world, which continues to live as if there is no God. Jesus' outward ministry was powerful, despite the real frustrations it encountered. But surrounding this new wine of His word and deed there was the wineskin of His parabolic life.

He also gave them this Comparison: "No housewife ever uses new, unshrunk material to patch an old dress. If she does, the new will shrink and pull, and won't match the old material. And nobody ever puts new, fermenting wine in old, brittle, plastic bottles. If he does, the new wine will pop the old bottles, and the wine will be wasted and the bottles ruined. But new wine is put into new, strong bottles." Luke 5:36-38.

The most tragic mistake we could make now would be to miss the point of this parable. The parables have been instilling new ideas within us. And we are trading with these ideas. But the ferment that is created by discipleship is too much for us to contain. We are like old, brittle, plastic bottles. How can we become new so that who we are is appropriate to what we say and what we do? What is the context out of which we show mercy and work for justice? Of course we do it in the context of this world, but there is a more immediate life situation which we have control over, which unifies and flavors our ministry, and which says something more powerful and more lasting than all of our separate words and deeds.

I remember vividly the Attica prison revolt in New York State a few years ago. I read a magazine account that was filled with brutal pictures. There were pictures of prisoners holding knives to the necks of their hostages and of helmeted grim-faced troops ready for the command to storm the cell block. There was a picture of several weary and rumpled officials trying to decide how to handle the uprising. Then there were the aftermath scenes of death and destruction. And in the midst of all this chaos and violence there was a single picture of a man in a pin-striped suit holding a press conference in an air-conditioned room miles away. He appeared to be well-rested, well-scrubbed, and well-fed. He was speaking in precise words to men and women sitting in neat rows of cushioned chairs. And he was telling them what happened at Attica. He was trying to convey the anguish of the story, complete with governmental recommendations on how to avoid future uprisings, but his lifestyle at that moment showed that he had not been personally involved. If there is any truth to the idea that the medium *is* the message, then his message was irrelevant.

We cannot talk of the kingdom of God if our lives symbolize the kingdom of this world. We may not talk in sterile proper terms of the cost of discipleship. There must be integrity between what we do and say — the new wine — and who we are — the new wineskin.

John the Baptist was such a good symbol of repentance that he didn't need to say much. Here comes this wild-eyed radical storming out of the desert, half-naked and half-starved, telling us we have to break with our old way of life. People understood what he meant because they saw him as a living message.

John's dress and diet were not a gimmick he contrived to get people's attention. Nor were they the subjects of his preaching. He did not try to impose his lifestyle upon others. His lifestyle was a natural accompaniment for his message. So if we want to get a handle on lifestyle — the medium — we need to look again at our message.

We represent, as Jesus did, the kingdom of God *over against* the kingdom of this world. *If there is no "over against," there is no kingdom of God*. We should not expect our lifestyle, in its totality, to reflect what is acceptable to this world, nor should it reflect the neutral ground that the two kingdoms have in common. Of course there are times when our mutual purposes permit us to cooperate with our culture. We do our best to live at peace with all, and we submit ourselves to the legitimate authority of the state. But the salt loses its taste when our peaceful coexistence with the world swallows up our resistance to the world. The preaching of the gospel includes much to which the world says "Amen," but the preaching of the gospel will eventually make you an outcast, lead you to prison, or force you underground. The kingdom of God invades and destroys the world by replacing systems of death and fear with justice and mercy.

When Jesus taught He spoke about a new order of the Spirit. When He healed He gave us an illustration of the abundant sufficiency of the new order. And when He went to the cross He acknowledged the absolute hostility between the old and the new. The cross is the wineskin. It is the inevitable culmination of the ministry of mercy and justice. It is the lifestyle of the kingdom of God as it exists within an alien culture. The cross represents the poverty of Jesus — the loss of His possessions, His friends, and His life. And it represents the nonviolent subversion of the world order.

The parabolic life is a life of eventual destitution and imprisonment. Do you suppose that you can be extravagant in your mercy without becoming poor? Do you suppose you can yell and pound and nag forever in your demand for justice for the oppressed without society eventually plotting how to get rid of you? If you compromise your way around the dispossession and alienation that the world imposes upon the children of grace, then you neutralize your works of mercy. The new wine is wasted.

We have moved now from the parables that Jesus spoke to the parable that Jesus lived. The word "parable" comes from two Greek words meaning "alongside of" and "to cast." A parable is a story, or a life, that is cast alongside of something else to highlight a specific point of similarity or distinction. Parables build bridges of enlightenment between the known and the unknown. Thus when Jesus told of the farmer who left the ninety-nine "found" sheep and sought the lost sheep, He was building a bridge between the farmer's action and the similar action of the Father in heaven. And when Jesus took the parable of the widow and the judge and threw it down alongside the social order of His day, He was revealing to us the world's reluctant concern for justice and the need for aggressive response to such callousness.

When Jesus cast His broken life alongside of the wholeness of the kingdom of God He provided a sharp visual contrast between the spiritual abundance and security of this kingdom and the emptiness of the kingdom of the world. When you analyze the joy of Jesus, you are driven to the conclusion that His joy came from doing the will of the Father. His strength could only have come from the Father. His forgiveness was divine. There was no earthly rationale for His compassion. He wasn't out to win votes or solicit funds. There were no hidden agendas, no strings attached. It was as if Jesus began by saying, "Blessed are the poor." Then He demonstrated what He meant. He said, "Blessed are the meek." Then His life defined the term. He told us that the last would be first, and we marveled at His words. Then He became last, and we beheld His glory. He *became* His message.

God cannot allow our witness to His kingdom to be blurred. People need to see us as symbols of a new humanity. When we say that we are citizens of the kingdom of God, we need to make that visible. If we choose the wineskin of a comfortable and secure life, we not only raise serious questions about our level of compassion, but we hide our light under a bushel. I believe there are other reasons, but if for no other reason than for the sake of clarity, we ought to renounce our citizenship in this world. We must avoid conflict of interest and the appearance of conflict of interest. If we are benefiting in terms of position, wealth, or power from a cozy relationship with the status quo, then we can't very well speak as representatives of a new world order. If we say that the joy of our fellowship with Christ is sufficient for us, then He ought to be our only source of joy. If we sing, "He's all I need," then He should be all we have.

We show that we believe in the promise of God when we put ourselves in that place where we have nothing to hold onto except for the promise of God.

Instead of trying to avoid the cross, we ought to welcome it. It is the best parable we have of the inherently hostile relationship that exists between the kingdom of God and the principalities and powers that rule our world. Our lives must in some ongoing creative way raise a clear witness to this hostility, or else mercy and justice are removed from their redemptive context.

Keep your eye peeled for fake preachers, who come to you with sheepskins from wolf-schools. You'll be able to distinguish them by the way they live. You know, you don't gather pecans from a persimmon tree nor peaches from a chinaberry, do you? So it is, a cultivated tree makes cultivated fruit, and a wild tree makes wild fruit. It is impossible for a cultivated tree to bear wild fruit, or for a wild tree to bear cultivated fruit. Any tree that does not produce cultivated fruit is chopped down and thrown into the fire. That's why I told you that you could know them by the way they *live*.

Not everyone who glibly calls me "Lord, Lord," shall enter the God Movement, but he who *does* the will of my spiritual Father. The time will come when many people will gather around and say, "L-o-ord, oh L-o-ord, *we* sure did preach in your name, didn't we? And in your name *we* gave the devil a run for his money, didn't we? *We* did all kinds of stunts in your name, didn't we?" Then I'll admit right in front of every-body, "I've never known you. Get away from me, you wicked religious racketeers."

That's why the man who hears these words of mine and acts on them shall be like a wise man who built his house on the rock. Down came the rain, up rose the floods, out lashed the winds. They all cut at that house, but it didn't fall. It was on *rock* foundation.

And the man who hears these words of mine and fails to act on them shall be like an idiot who built his house on the sand. The rain came down, the floods rose up, the winds lashed out. They all cut at that house, and it fell! And my, what a collapse! Matthew 7:15-27.

Who are the "fake preachers"? They are those who preach the gospel out of context. They talk about the good news and the changed life, but their own lives demonstrate that the demands of God allow for conformity to old allegiance. Who are the ones who say "Lord, Lord"? They are not pagans. They are "Christians" — Christians, in fact, who do the works that normally demonstrate the power of the kingdom of God. But mercy has become a "stunt." Justice has been absorbed into the normal flow of cultural event. The status quo hasn't been shattered. The peace hasn't been disturbed There has been no "over against." And the kingdom hasn't come.

Who are the "wise" ones who build their lives upon the rock? They are the ones who have put God's ideas into action, and who have

153

surrounded those ideas with a parabolic life. Through its servanthood and resistance, the parabolic life points out that things are not as they should be. And a foretaste of a new emerging world is provided.

God "knows" us when we enter His family, not when we are content with a superficial imitation of His family traits. The parables have given us at best some passing entertainment, and at worst a rough ride that is happily ended, *unless* we build our homes upon their truth. Perhaps we have listened, and listened, without catching on. But if our eyes have seen, and our ears have heard, and our hearts have understood, then we have been turned around. The parables have led us into the kingdom of God, and our lives become a fresh incarnation of His nature.

NOTES

Author's Preface

1. The story of Clarence Jordan and the Koinonia Farm experiment is recorded in *The Cotton Patch Evidence*, by Dallas Lee (New York: Harper and Row, 1971).

2. Dallas Lee, editor (New York: Association Press, 1971).

Prologue

1. Dorothy Kalins, *Cutting Loose — A Civilized Guide for Getting Out of the System* (New York: Saturday Review Press, 1973).

Chaper 2

1. Clarence called the parables "Comparisons" because they compared an aspect of common experience with an otherwise obscure aspect of spiritual truth.

Chapter 3

1. It is significant that the Greek word for judgment is *crisis*.

2. John 8:32.

3. Matthew 21:45-46; Luke 20:19.

4. This translation is one that Clarence made directly from the Greek text during a talk. It is not identical to his published Cotton Patch version.

5. Luke 13:30; Matthew 19:30 and 20:16; Mark 10:31. *Cf*. Luke 14:11 and 18:14; Matthew 23:12.

6. To be a literate American is strong circumstantial evidence that one is "on top."

7. 2 Samuel 11:1 — 12:15.

Chapter 4

1. I agree with Clarence that not all people are in actuality children of God and, therefore, not all are in actuality brothers and sisters, even though they should be and could be. Nevertheless, at other places in this book I will refer to our "brothers and sisters," meaning all of our fellow humans. I do not intend to blur the distinction between the actual and the ideal, but only to reinforce the intention that God has for us. We should not call ourselves "brothers and sisters" when there is great disparity between the circumstances of our lives. But we need to see ourselves as brothers and sisters in order to be reconciled to each other and God.

2. In the original Cotton Patch version, Clarence refers to the "drachma," the Greek word, as a "dime." I have changed it to "penny" to make the translation conform to the commentary that he gave at a later time. Perhaps we can credit the difference to inflation!

3. "Healthy people don't need a doctor — only the sick do. I haven't come to challenge the 'saved' people to a new way of walking — only the 'sinners' " (Luke 5:31-32).

4. It was undoubtedly offensive to Jesus' hearers, as it may be to us, that God is portrayed as a woman.

5. Luke 4:16-30.

6. This is actually the modern-day equivalent of what Jesus did say, and if you are a member of such a church, your response to Jesus' statement may conform to the response of the Nazareth congregation.

7. Luke 19:47.

Chapter 5

1. This commentary on the rich farmer is taken from the record, "The Great Banquet and Other Parables," retold by Clarence Jordan and produced by Koinonia Records.

Chapter 6

1. "Yahweh, who does what is right, is always on the side of the oppressed" (Psalm 103:6, *Jerusalem Bible*).

2. The term "third world" normally refers to the underdeveloped nations of Africa, Asia, and Latin America. It may, as in this case, refer to impoverished people anywhere.

3. The word for "rock" in the Greek is *petros*, or Peter. Jesus, as Clarence's translation points out, gave Simon the nickname "Rock" in Matthew 16:18.

4. In the above Cotton Patch version I have altered Clarence's use of personal pronouns to more accurately reflect the substance and intent of the Greek text.

5. Romans 13 develops this idea of the state as God's agent for the ordering of society along just lines. The nation as God's instrument for justice is to that extent ordained by God.

6. It is possible, as we shall discuss later, that the state will decide to get rid of us in a more unpleasant manner. After Jesus created a ruckus in the Temple, the state and religious authorities conspired together to destroy Him. Luke 19:45-48.

7. Micah 6:6-8; Matthew 9:13.

Chapter 7

1. Genesis 3:1-7.

2. The "church member" and the "unsaved man" of the Cotton Patch version are the "Pharisee" and the "Publican" of the Greek text, and in this commentary, taken from *The Substance of Faith*, pp. 139-140, Clarence reverts to the literal terminology.

3. Luke 3:8.

Chapter 8

1. Luke 15:2 speaks literally of the Pharisees and scribes.

2. I have altered Clarence's use of personal pronouns to more accurately reflect the Greek text.

3. Some of the Jews, who had toiled through the heat of the day, apparently resented Jesus' extension of mercy to the Gentiles, who had not suffered through the Old Testament agonies of Israel.

4. We notice in this passage from Luke that Jesus is once again lashing out at the propriety and timidity that keep us from entering the kingdom.

Chapter 9

1. Paul said, "I live *every* day on death row" (1 Corinthians 15:31).

Chapter 10

1. The Cotton Patch version uses sums of money to symbolize the investment that Jesus, the businessman in the parable, has made in His "assistants." In the Greek, a "talent" refers to a large amount of money.

2. Matthew 5:11-12.

3. Amos 5:24.
4. Matthew 5:13-16.
5. Philippians 3:10, *Jerusalem Bible*

Chapter 11

1. Literally he was a Samaritan. The Samaritans and Jews often discriminated against each other in Jesus' day because they were of different races.

2. Jesus said that God would confirm His will to us while we were in the process of carrying it out. John 7:17.

Chapter 12

1. Luke 17:12-19.

2. Matthew 21:12-17. Jesus' defiant act did not mark the end of the exploitation of the poor in the name of religion.

3. John 11:1-44.

CLARENCE JORDAN is widely known for his Cotton Patch Version of the New Testament and as founder of Koinonia, an interracial farming community at Americus, Georgia, in the heart of the deep South.

Recognized as a compelling and dramatic speaker, Jordan addressed many church conferences and conventions. He died on October 29, 1969, while preparing a speech to deliver the next day at Mercer University, Macon, Georgia.

Born to a prominent family in Talbotton, Georgia, Jordan held a BS degree in agriculture from the University of Georgia and ThM and PhD degrees in New Testament Greek from Southern Baptist Seminary, Louisville, Kentucky.

Four children, now all married, were born to Clarence and his wife, Florence (Kroeger): Eleanor Kroeger, James Frederick, Janet Elizabeth, and Frank Leonard.

Jordan's published works include: *The Cotton Patch Version of Matthew and John, The Cotton Patch Version of Luke and Acts, The Cotton Patch Version of Paul's Epistles, The Cotton Patch Version of Hebrews and the General Epistles,* and *The Substance of Faith and Other Cotton Patch Sermons* (all by Association Press), and *Sermon on the Mount* (Judson Press).

Various records and cassettes of Clarence Jordan speaking in his pungent and inimitable style are available from Koinonia Partners, Route 2, Americus, GA 31709.

BILL LANE DOULOS has been a friend of Koinonia since his first visit there in 1970. He is a former member of their board of directors. Bill spent three years as a staff instructor for Young Life Campaign in Pittsburgh, Pennsylvania, and later was a full-time staff person for All Saints Episcopal Church, Pasadena, California, providing social services to the poor. Currently he is a PhD student at the University of Southern California, School of Religion, majoring in social ethics.

William Lane and Sybil Flanagan were married in 1971. Later both took the surname Doulos (a Greek word meaning servant or slave) to symbolize their oneness, equality, and common aspirations. They have kept their former surnames as middle names to maintain family ties. Sybil is a registered nurse working in pediatrics. Bill and Sybil are the parents of a young daughter, Melissa Lucy.

Three booklets published under Bill's former name are available from Koinonia: *The Christian and Materialism*, *The Radical Church*, and *The Christian Radical*. He is corresponding editor for *Sojourners* magazine (formerly the *Post-American*).

Born at Johnstown, Pennsylvania, Bill attended the Mt. Lebanon, Pennsylvania, public schools. He holds a BA degree in English from Westminster College, New Wilmington, Pennsylvania; attended Gordon Divinity School, Wenham, Massachusetts; and holds an MDiv degree from Fuller Theological Seminary, Pasadena, California.